"Chapman and Gratz expand the boundaries of dialectical behavior therapy (DBT) and provide readers with a practical blueprint for managing destructive and excessive anger reactions. A must-read for anyone interested in reducing problematic anger, improving relationships, and enhancing inner peace."

—**Raymond Chip Tafrate, PhD**, professor and clinical psychologist in the department of criminology and criminal justice at Central Connecticut State University, coeditor of *Forensic CBT*, and coauthor of *Anger Management for Everyone*

"Anger is an emotion that we all experience in varying degrees. However, intense and poorly modulated anger can greatly interfere with clients' efforts at a central goal of dialectical behavior therapy (DBT): 'building a life worth living.' This compassionately written and motivating workbook is an essential resource for helping clients to understand, express, and effectively manage their anger in nondestructive ways. By teaching clients to apply core DBT skills specifically to help them cope with and manage their anger, this book is an indispensable and potentially life-changing therapeutic tool."

—**Lori N. Scott, PhD**, assistant professor of psychiatry at the University of Pittsburgh School of Medicine, and clinical psychologist and researcher with expertise in emotion dysregulation, aggression, and treatment approaches for borderline personality disorder

"Anyone who gets angry will benefit from learning the skills in this highly readable yet scientifically sound book."

—**Ruth Baer, PhD**, professor of psychology at the University of Kentucky, and author of *The Practicing Happiness Workbook*

T0304928

"Chapman and Gratz have tackled the significant human challenge of anger and provide a much-needed, easy-to-follow, step-by-step guide to making anger 'an ally rather than an enemy.' They provide skillful guidance in better understanding, recognizing, and responding to our own angry responses so that anger does not disrupt our lives. Their practical, compassionate approach will help clients (and therapists who work with them) to learn new skills for managing their anger, including how to express it effectively and how to recover following angry interactions. I highly recommend this book to anyone who struggles with anger, and to those committed to helping them lead more satisfying lives."

—**Lizabeth Roemer, PhD**, professor of psychology at the University of Massachusetts Boston, and coauthor of *The Mindful Way through Anxiety*

"*The Dialectical Behavior Therapy Skills Workbook for Anger* by Chapman and Gratz uses current dialectical behavior therapy (DBT) emotion theory and behavioral principles to create a practical, easy-to-read guidebook for managing unhelpful anger. Complex theory is broken down—step-by-step—into principles of change and then translated into realistic skills and user-friendly worksheets. This manual is a must-read for anyone struggling with how to understand, express, or regulate anger."

—**Thomas R. Lynch, PhD, FBPsS**, professor and director of the School of Psychology and director of the Emotion and Personality Bio-behavioural Laboratory at the University of Southampton, as well as chief investigator at REFRAMED

"Dysregulated anger is a major part of the emotional instability dimension of borderline personality disorder (BPD). This skills workbook by Chapman and Gratz presents clients, in enriched detail, an abundant array of techniques, self-learning schemes, and practical exercises to enhance anger control capacity. Well done."

—**Raymond W. Novaco, PhD**, professor at the University of California, Irvine

"In *The Dialectical Behavior Therapy Skills Workbook for Anger*, authors Chapman and Gratz present a nuanced view of anger, pointing out the benefits as well as the pitfalls of this complex and vexing emotion. The authors provide a thorough education on anger, beginning with a useful description of the many diagnoses and clinical presentations that anger often accompanies. They then walk readers through the components of anger, vulnerability factors for anger, keys to recognizing anger, and consequences of anger. They include strategies for increasing commitment to changing it, describe a range of dialectical behavior therapy (DBT) skills for reducing it, provide methods to express it appropriately, offer ways of changing thinking that fuels it, and, importantly, suggest ways to repair relationships after inevitable anger 'slipups' occur. The book includes relevant case vignettes and numerous easy-to-use worksheets that help readers engage with and apply the material. Chapman and Gratz have produced a work in easy-to-understand, clear language that makes behavior therapy principles and DBT skills for the emotion of anger readily accessible to readers. I highly recommend their insightful and helpful book!"

—**Jill Rathus, PhD**, professor of psychology at the C.W. Post Campus of
    Long Island University, and codirector of Cognitive Behavioral Associates
    in Great Neck, NY

"This is a reader-friendly resource with practical and straightforward solutions to problems managing anger. Adapted from dialectical behavior therapy (DBT), these contemporary cognitive and behavioral skills are sure to transform lives by helping people learn to predict and control responses across the spectrum of anger, from the mildest of irritation to the extremes of rage."

—**M. Zachary Rosenthal, PhD**, associate professor, vice chair of clinical services,
    and director of the Cognitive-Behavioral Research and Treatment Program,
    departments of psychiatry and behavioral sciences and psychology and
    neuroscience, Duke University

The Dialectical Behavior Therapy Skills Workbook

— *for* —

Anger

Using DBT Mindfulness & Emotion
Regulation Skills to Manage Anger

ALEXANDER L. CHAPMAN, PhD, RPsych
KIM L. GRATZ, PhD

New Harbinger Publications, Inc.

Publisher's Note

This publication is designed to provide accurate and authoritative information in regard to the subject matter covered. It is sold with the understanding that the publisher is not engaged in rendering psychological, financial, legal, or other professional services. If expert assistance or counseling is needed, the services of a competent professional should be sought.

This book is independently authored and published and is not endorsed or sponsored by or affiliated with any third party, including the various individuals and organizations who use the acronym DBT or the phrase Dialectical Behavior Therapy in their trademarks. Both of these terms are used in this book strictly in their generic meanings to identify a form of therapy that is utilized by many scholars and practitioners in the field of psychology. By way of example, this book is not endorsed by or affiliated in any way with Dr. Marsha M. Linehan, who is recognized as a pioneer in the field of Dialectical Behavior Therapy and who offers her professional services under the federally registered trademark DBT.

NEW HARBINGER PUBLICATIONS is a registered trademark of New Harbinger Publications, Inc.

Distributed in Canada by Raincoast Books

Copyright © 2015 by Alexander L. Chapman and Kim L. Gratz
New Harbinger Publications, Inc.
5674 Shattuck Avenue
Oakland, CA 94609
www.newharbinger.com

All Rights Reserved

Acquired by Catharine Meyers; Cover design by Amy Shoup; Edited by James Lainsbury

---

Library of Congress Cataloging-in-Publication Data

Chapman, Alexander L. (Alexander Lawrence)
    The dialectical behavior therapy skills workbook for anger : using DBT mindfulness and emotion regulation skills to manage anger / Alexander L. Chapman, Kim L. Gratz.
        pages cm
    Includes bibliographical references.
    ISBN 978-1-62625-021-5 (paperback) -- ISBN 978-1-62625-022-2 (pdf e-book) -- ISBN 978-1-62625-023-9 (epub)
1. Anger--Treatment. 2. Dialectical behavior therapy. I. Gratz, Kim L. II. Title.
    RC569.5.A53C43 2015
    616.89'142--dc23
                            2015020073

Printed in the United States of America

23 22 21

15 14 13 12

To the clients in my DBT skills group. You continue to inspire me with your incredible capacity for growth.

—Alexander L. Chapman

To all the clients to whom I have taught DBT skills. You have taught and inspired me in many ways.

—Kim L. Gratz

Contents

Acknowledgments

First and foremost, I am incredibly grateful to the clients who have taught and inspired me so much. In particular, I think often of those of you in my DBT skills group and look forward to seeing you every week. I'd like to express appreciation for my wonderful mentors, colleagues, and friends who have helped me grow as a psychologist and have provided incredible support and encouragement over the years, including Dr. Richard Farmer, Tony Cellucci, Thomas R. Lynch, Clive Robins, and Marsha Linehan. Kim Gratz, with whom I wrote this book (and several others), has been such a wonderful friend and colleague over the years. I have always thoroughly enjoyed our writing projects, and I learn new things whenever we work together. Thank you to the dedicated editorial staff at New Harbinger, especially Catharine Meyers and Jess Beebe, and freelance editor James Lainsbury. Last but not least, I'm incredibly grateful for my wonderful, loving family, including my lovely wife, Katherine, my two sons, Max and Quinn, and my parents, who have always supported me in everything I do.

—Alexander L. Chapman

I am extremely grateful to the clients who have shared their journeys toward recovery with me. They bring these skills to life and keep this treatment new and exciting. They are forever teaching me new ways of thinking about these skills and sharing this information with others. I am also extraordinarily grateful to the mentors who trained me and continue to support me throughout my career, including Drs. Liz Roemer, John Gunderson, and Elizabeth Murphy. My career would not be possible without their support, encouragement, and guidance along the way. As always, I am also grateful to my dear friend and colleague Alex Chapman, without whom these books would not be possible. There is no one with whom I would rather write these books, and the process is far more enjoyable (and tolerable!) as a result of our collaboration. I also remain thankful for the dedicated editorial staff at New Harbinger, especially Catharine Meyers, Jess Beebe, and freelance editor James Lainsbury.

My deepest gratitude goes to those who sustain and nurture me on a daily basis, particularly my husband, partner, best friend, and amazing collaborator, Matt Tull. His love, support (emotional and practical), wisdom, and willingness to care for me make everything possible—this book, my career, and my happiness. Finally, I will always be grateful to my parents, Linda and Dave, for their unconditional love and support throughout my life, and to Daisy for bringing unfathomable love, joy, and peace into our lives.

—Kim L. Gratz

Foreword

Dialectical Behavior Therapy (DBT) is an emotion-focused, skills-oriented treatment. When I began to develop DBT more than three decades ago, one of the first lessons I learned was that difficulty managing emotions played a crucial role in the suffering of many of my clients. Likely due to a combination of social and biological factors, the clients I worked with did not have the skills they needed to manage emotions. Their emotions were frightening, overwhelmingly intense, and felt out of control. Emotions—in particular anger—often led to dysfunctional behaviors that could only make matters worse. As a result, my clients would often try desperately to escape their pain by engaging in self-injury, suicide attempts, or other self-damaging behaviors. Dealing with emotions felt a lot like trying to fly a fighter jet with little or no training; it seemed like the only option was to press the parachute button. And one of the hardest emotions to manage was anger. DBT skills were developed to teach clients how to regulate emotions, including anger.

This book, *The DBT Skills Workbook for Anger*, focuses on anger, and as you read it you will find that anger is a fascinating emotion. Intense anger can be a powerful and overwhelming experience. It charges us up and makes us feel like taking action. One of the problems with anger is that some of the actions we feel like doing when we're angry end up making things worse. Yelling and acting in an aggressive, harsh, critical, or demanding manner can be damaging to relationships, make it hard to keep a job, and make already stressful situations worse. Chronic resentment and hostility can make life miserable and even lead to health problems. Yet, when managed effectively, anger can help us get things done, stand up for our rights or the rights of others, seek justice, and change stressful situations. Maximizing the potential of anger takes a fair amount of skill. That's where this workbook comes in.

In this workbook, Alex Chapman and Kim Gratz take a nonjudgmental approach that promotes acceptance and understanding, while providing practical tips on how to regulate anger using DBT skills. The earlier chapters package the latest research on emotions and anger in a way that is easily understandable and usable. Alex and Kim frame anger as part of our body and brain's natural defense system (the flight-flight-freeze system) and clearly describe the types of physical sensations, thoughts, and actions that go along with anger. The ability to label emotions is a critical DBT skill particularly important when trying to manage anger, an emotion many people refuse to admit. They also include an excellent chapter on how to get (and remain) motivated to work on anger, using strategies that DBT and other therapists use to help enhance their clients' motivation. Taking the first few steps in effectively managing our anger, however, doesn't just require motivation; it also requires understanding of our patterns of anger. Alex and Kim provide exercises to help the reader do just this.

This workbook includes several excellent chapters anchored by DBT skills that systematically help the reader deal with anger. Some of the chapters provide suggestions on how to reduce vulnerability to anger, and how to use mindfulness skills to ride out urges to act on anger. Other chapters provide practical suggestions, from the DBT distress tolerance skills, on how to avoid making situations worse when angry. Using some of the latest DBT skills (Linehan, 2015), Alex and Kim also guide the reader in how to dampen the physical sensations of anger, deal with angry thoughts, act opposite to anger, and manage the some of the after-effects of anger episodes. Instead of framing anger as an emotion to squash, suppress, or get rid of, Alex and Kim provide readers with guidance on how to effectively express anger, using DBT interpersonal effectiveness skills. This combination of skills oriented toward accepting and changing anger nicely embodies the spirit of DBT.

Not only is this workbook practical, compassionate, and nonjudgmental, it is also based on solid scientific evidence on the treatment of anger. Both DBT as a full-treatment package (including individual therapy, group skills training, telephone consultation, and the DBT consultation team) and DBT skills training have consistently shown large effects in the treatment of anger (e.g., see Lieb et al., 2004; Robins & Chapman, 2004; Stoffers et al., 2012). Many of the DBT skills directly come from what we know about effective cognitive behavioral treatments (CBTs), and recent reviews have shown that CBT has consistently strong evidence and large effects in the treatment of anger (Hoffman et al., 2012). Therefore, readers of this book can be confident that the advice offered comes from sound scientific evidence.

—Marsha M. Linehan, PhD, ABPP

Introduction and Overview

Anger is a fascinating and important emotion. It can add passion and energy to our lives, giving us an electrifying jolt that helps us protect ourselves, fight injustice and unfairness, defend our rights, and confront those who are mistreating us. Despite its usefulness, anger can also be incredibly frustrating, arriving like an unwelcome guest who crashes the party. It can be a major roadblock, getting in the way of our lives, relationships, and jobs. Regardless of whether we love or hate anger, hold on to it or fear it, anger is almost always captivating. And rest assured, we all experience it.

If you are reading this book, then it is likely that you struggle with anger. If this is the case, it is important for you to know that you're not alone. Anger causes difficulties in many people's lives, including with their jobs, their relationships, and even their physical health. One study found that 15 percent of participants had very high scores on a measure of hostility (Romanov et al. 1994), and a 2003 survey found that more than one-third of adult drivers reported having been shouted at or cursed at while driving (Smart, Mann, and Stoduto 2003). Furthermore, research on anger has shown that chronic anger and hostility can increase one's vulnerability to cardiovascular problems (Suls and Bunde 2005), cause problems in relationships, pose barriers to functioning at work, and get in the way of important goals (Kassinove 1995).

Although there is no official "anger disorder" in the *Diagnostic and Statistical Manual of Mental Disorders*, fifth edition (American Psychiatric Association 2013), the guide used in North America for diagnosing psychiatric disorders, anger is a feature of many psychiatric problems. It is a feature of borderline personality disorder (BPD), post-traumatic stress disorder, conduct disorder, oppositional defiant disorder, intermittent explosive disorder (in which people engage in bursts of aggressive behavior), and others. Even depression and grief often are accompanied by feelings of anger. Although many people think that euphoria, energy, and a feeling of being on top of the world are the most important features of mania (a symptom of bipolar disorder), it is actually more common for people to feel angry and irritable when they are manic. In addition, when couples seek help for relationship problems, anger often has played an important role in their difficulties.

It's also important to keep in mind that even people who do not have serious problems with anger or a specific psychiatric disorder can still fall victim to the throes of anger from time to time. This can take the form of an unintended snippy remark to a loved one, driving in an unsafe manner, sending an angry message, yelling at someone, or making snap decisions. Indeed, managing anger can feel like trying to control a large and restless animal.

Keep in mind, though, that anger can also be one of your strongest allies. If people didn't feel angry about discrimination and the mistreatment of others, they might never take action against social injustice. On a more personal level, if you feel anger or indignation when someone mistreats you, those feelings can spur you to action to stop the mistreatment. If someone threatened you physically and you didn't feel angry at all, you might not be as able to defend yourself. Anger can be an extremely motivating and energizing emotion, giving you the fuel you need to break through barriers, persist, and work hard to achieve a goal. The goal, then, is not to get rid of anger, but to understand it and learn to manage and use it to achieve what's important to you.

We wrote this book to help you understand anger and to learn how to effectively manage it using skills from dialectical behavior therapy (Linehan 1993a). We have pulled together what we know from the scientific study of anger, from effective treatments for anger, and from our own experiences with clients who struggle with anger. Wherever possible, we include exercises to help you practice the skills and strategies we discuss, and we encourage you to think about whether what we discuss throughout this book applies to your own unique situation.

DIALECTICAL BEHAVIOR THERAPY

Before you start reading the rest of the chapters, we'd like to first give you a little information about dialectical behavior therapy (DBT). We expand on this topic in chapter 2. For now, know that DBT is a treatment that includes several parts:

- Weekly individual therapy (usually for about an hour)

- A weekly skills training group (usually for about two hours) in which clients learn skills in the areas of mindfulness, emotion regulation, distress tolerance, and interpersonal effectiveness

- A therapist who is available for between-session phone calls focused on how to apply coping skills in real life

- A team approach to therapy, consisting of weekly meetings between therapists who support each other in their efforts to do the best possible work with clients

Dr. Marsha Linehan, a professor at the University of Washington, developed DBT to help clients who had complex mental health problems. These people had attempted suicide many times and couldn't see a way out of their suffering. Many of them struggled with intense and overwhelming emotions, such as shame, fear, anxiety, sadness, and, of course, anger.

DBT works especially well to help people manage their emotions. Indeed, over the last couple of decades researchers have found DBT to be a very effective treatment for people with complex mental health problems, such as borderline personality disorder (BPD). People who suffer from BPD have many problems, including difficulty managing emotions, rocky and stormy relationships, and confusion about identity. One of the symptoms of BPD is intense anger, which is marked by difficulty controlling anger (American Psychiatric Association 2013). There is consistent evidence across studies suggesting that DBT helps people suffering from BPD to reduce their anger (Stoffers et al. 2012).

You should know that you don't have to have BPD to benefit from DBT. DBT includes several practical and easy-to-learn skills and strategies to help all sorts of people understand, accept, and regulate intense emotions, including anger. In fact, we often hear clients say that they wish elementary schools and high schools taught DBT skills because they are so useful for so many aspects of life. We believe that these skills and strategies will become invaluable to you in your efforts to overcome your anger, and that is why we focus on DBT in this book.

HOW TO USE THIS BOOK

Probably the most helpful way to navigate the book is to read it from start to finish. The earlier chapters offer background on anger, providing a solid foundation that makes it easier to use the skills discussed in later chapters. If you already know a fair bit about anger and your own triggers and patterns, you may want to zero in on a chapter that covers the skills you need most. The summaries of each chapter below should help you decide how you'd like to proceed.

- Chapter 1 covers some of what the field of psychology knows about emotions, how to understand anger, and the different components of anger.

- Chapter 2 provides a summary of DBT and the various DBT skills covered in this book.

- Chapter 3 helps you find ways to get motivated (and stay motivated) to work on your anger.

- Chapter 4 helps you learn how to identify and understand your patterns of anger.

- Chapter 5 addresses ways to reduce your vulnerability to anger by improving your self-care.

- Chapter 6 describes the use of mindfulness skills to ride out and experience anger without acting on it.

- Chapter 7 offers skills to help you avoid acting on your anger and making a situation worse.

- Chapter 8 reviews relaxation, intense exercise, self-soothing, and other strategies to help reduce the physical experience of anger.

- Chapter 9 includes skills to help you effectively manage the thoughts that arise when you're angry.

- Chapter 10 focuses on the skill of opposite action, which will help you behave differently when you're angry.

- Chapter 11 discusses ways to effectively express anger.

- Chapter 12 addresses ways to recover from anger episodes and to repair relationships after the inevitable slipup.

Once you start incorporating the skills in this book into your everyday life, situations that used to blow up and result in guilt, shame, and embarrassment can be transformed. Understanding and effectively managing anger can make an enormous difference in your life and your relationships, helping you get closer to important goals. Moreover, when you begin to notice that you're having fewer anger flare-ups and that you're better equipped to cope with them, you should start to feel more confident and enjoy a greater sense of peace in your daily life.

Moving Forward

We are excited to share with you what we know about anger and how to effectively cope with it. We work with clients and their anger problems, teach students and clinicians how to do effective therapy, and do research on how people manage emotions. This book is a wonderful opportunity to use what we have learned in both our professional and personal lives to help you make anger an ally rather than an enemy. In order to do that, you first need to have a solid understanding of what anger is, and that's what we talk about in chapter 1. Let's get started!

CHAPTER 1

Understanding Anger
from the Inside Out

Just as you wouldn't want to jump in and try to fix your car without any mechanical knowledge, it is important to first understand what anger is and how it works before trying to fix or change it. Of course, human beings are much more complex than cars, so you probably won't be surprised to learn that psychologists know a lot less about what anger is and how it works than mechanics know about cars. Emotions are a lot more enigmatic than pistons, spark plugs, and fuel injectors. Nonetheless, going over what we do know about anger is a helpful place to start. This information will help you learn how to effectively deal with anger.

ANGER AS AN EMOTION

Let's start by talking about anger as an emotion. Emotions are universal. We all have them. In fact, scientists have found that around the world, people from different cultures, backgrounds, races, and walks of life experience a common set of emotions. These include anger, sadness, happiness, fear, disgust, shame, guilt, jealousy, and envy, among others. The responses to many of these emotions are so consistent around the world that we can identify them simply by looking at facial expressions.

Each emotion has many varieties. Anger-related emotions range from mild annoyance to frustration or aggravation to intense rage. You don't always feel the most intense form of any emotion. For example, one day your anger might come in the form of frequent feelings of irritation and annoyance, whereas the next day it could manifest as intense spikes of rage.

Why do emotions exist in the first place? Many researchers think that emotions evolved to help us survive, functioning a lot like a very sophisticated, sensitive life-support system. When your heartbeat slows down or your blood oxygen levels drop in a hospital, a life-support system has lights and alarms that signal if something is wrong. In a similar way, negative emotions such as anger, fear, or anxiety are reactions that tell you when something might be wrong. For example, you could be in danger, someone could be mistreating you, or there may be a problem to solve. Physical sensations, such as a racing heartbeat, tense muscles, and perspiration, are like the beeps and alarms of a life-support system.

Unlike life-support systems, which are set up only to detect danger, emotions also tell you when something good is happening. Happiness and contentment can be signals that what you're doing is good for you. Excitement might be telling you that something great is happening. Feelings of love might tell you that you admire or feel safe and close to someone, and that spending more time with that person could be good for you. As you can see, emotions are very useful, helping us avoid harm and move toward things that are beneficial.

Another important thing to know about emotions, including anger, is that they don't last very long (Gross 2014). Emotions are temporary reactions to events that happen to us; sometimes they are reactions to the thoughts we're having. Emotions are different from what we refer to as "moods." Moods last longer and do not change much in response to what's happening to us. An emotion is a lot like the weather on a particular day, whereas moods are a lot like the climate.

So, what do we know about anger as an emotional state? We know that anger is temporary. It flares up for a brief period and then dies down. Like other emotional states, anger does not last forever—or even very long. If we allow anger to run its course and get away from the thing provoking our anger, it will pass fairly quickly.

Sometimes we experience anger that doesn't go away quickly. Perhaps you've had a day during which every little thing bothered you, and you felt kind of keyed up and edgy. This general feeling of irritability, lasting several hours or longer, is what we call a mood, whereas the small spikes of irritation or anger that flare up in reaction to specific events—such as being cut off while driving, missing a bus, or being told that you should've cleaned the kitchen more thoroughly—and die down quickly are emotional states.

Though they are fairly temporary, emotions are quite complex, involving both the body and brain. It has often been said that emotions come from the heart, whereas logic and thinking come from the brain. This makes sense because you might first notice an emotion in your body. Perhaps your heart is racing, your palms are sweaty, and your muscles are tense. It might seem like emotions are only experiences of the body, whereas thinking is localized in the brain—emotions are in your "heart" but thoughts are in your "mind." As it turns out, the body and brain are essentially one and the same. Perhaps this fact is most truly expressed in an emotional response. An emotion is not just how you feel but a whole body-brain response. When an emotion fires, your brain, nervous system, muscles, heart, and blood chemistry are all involved.

ANGER AND AGGRESSION

It is important to remember that emotions and actions are related but different. A lot of people associate anger with aggression, and the two can be related, but they're not the same thing. Aggression involves actions or statements that might be harmful to someone or something, whereas anger is an *emotional state*. You can feel very angry and frustrated, enraged even, but still not act aggressively. Similarly, people can act aggressively when they're not angry or frustrated. For example, the last time the Vancouver Canucks came close to winning the Stanley Cup (the holy grail in hockey) and lost, many fans went downtown and rioted. They smashed and burned cars, broke windows, were insulting toward police, and worse. Some of these folks may have been angry and upset that their team lost, but the videos of the riot suggest otherwise. Many of the rioters were laughing and jumping around. They looked like they were at a party having a lot of fun.

As another example, consider boxing or martial arts. By definition, sparring and boxing matches are aggressive; often the goal is to immobilize or knock out your opponent. And yet neither competitor would be likely to say that anger had anything to do with it. Indeed, if these fighters were fitfully angry, they probably wouldn't be thinking clearly enough to defend themselves.

The main point to keep in mind is that anger and aggression are not one and the same. In fact, for years researchers have debated about the role of anger or frustration in aggressive behavior (Kassinove 1995). And this lack of clear connection is very good news. Just because you feel angry doesn't mean that you need to or will act aggressively. You have the freedom to do something else, something more life enhancing and effective.

WHEN DO WE FEEL ANGRY?

Many people who study anger believe that in order to feel angry we need to be aware that something negative or undesirable is happening to us (Deffenbacher 1999; Kassinove 1995). The first important point is that you're unlikely to feel anger (or any other emotion) about an event you're not aware of. If somebody says really negative things about you behind your back but you never find out, you will not react with anger. If you remain asleep while your home is robbed, you will not experience fear because you are not aware there are robbers in your home. Our brains somehow need to become aware of an event in order for us to have an emotional reaction.

The second important point is that human beings don't tend to feel angry about just any event. For anger to happen, we have to experience or view an event as negative, unpleasant, or undesirable. Why and how do we experience events as negative, unpleasant, or undesirable? In the case of emotions, it's helpful to remember that many researchers believe that emotions evolved to help us survive and reach important goals. As a result, emotions tend to arise when a situation seems relevant to some important goal or desire (Mauss et al. 2005). Imagine your goal is to get into graduate school, for which you need excellent grades, but you think your professor marked an exam unfairly. You might see this grade and, by extension, the situation as getting in the way of your goal. Perhaps they also get in the way of your desire to be treated fairly and with respect. If a large bear walks into your office, part of the reason you feel so afraid is that your brain perceives the bear as a threat to your goals of survival and avoiding harm. In general, emotions such as anger arise when you perceive a situation as being bad for you in relation to your goals (Ochsner and Gross 2014).

It is important to remember that you don't always have to think carefully about something before you have an emotional reaction to it. Often your brain notices very quickly whether something is good or bad for you. In fact, this often happens in areas of your brain that are not involved in deep thinking or the processing of information, such as the amygdala (Ochsner and Gross 2014). Think about what would happen if we had to spend time thinking carefully about each oncoming car when crossing a street. *Hmm… Let me think about this. The car seems to be getting bigger and bigger. I deduce that this means the car is getting closer to me in a rapid fashion.* Bam! A lot more of us would get hit. Perceiving a situation as good or bad can occur very quickly, which can help us do what's needed right away. Indeed, the beauty of our emotional system is its quickness and efficiency.

Of course, for many of us the speed of an emotional response is one of the most maddening things about emotions such as anger. Sometimes you might feel like your anger goes from zero to sixty miles per hour in a split second. It might seem like there's really no room to think, plan, or manage your anger before you do or say something that you regret. The good news, however, is that our brains are constantly learning and changing. We can learn to slow down and consciously choose our actions, and some of the skills in this book will help you do just that. We can also learn new ways of reacting to the very same situations that used to drive us crazy. Even if these same situations still get under our skin and lead to very intense anger, we can learn to act in ways that are more consistent with our personal values and goals. We can learn how to manage our anger so that it doesn't stay as intense for as long. We discuss many of these strategies in this book, and if you practice them regularly, we are confident that you will be able to more effectively manage your anger.

Now that it's clear that anger is an emotional reaction to things we experience as negative, unpleasant, or undesirable, it might be helpful to explore the types of events that tend to make people angry.

Cues for Anger. A *cue* is something that sets the stage for an emotional response. Keep in mind that everyone is different. What makes you angry may not make someone else angry. Broadly speaking, there are a few common cues for anger:

- Situations we perceive as threatening

- Being prevented or blocked from reaching an important goal

- Unpleasant physical sensations and physical and emotional pain

Anger is a common reaction when someone threatens your physical or emotional well-being or the well-being of loved ones. For example, many people would feel quite angry if someone insulted them in a room full of people. This kind of behavior could be considered a threat to one's emotional well-being or status. It is also common to feel angry when somebody mistreats, insults, threatens, or is rude to someone we care about or love. Many of us would also feel intense anger (and probably fear) if somebody behaved in a physically aggressive or threatening manner toward us. Threats to identity, competence, or integrity are also cues for anger (Lazarus 1991).

Being prevented from reaching a goal is another common cue for anger. For example, when you're already running late for work and the person in front of you is driving particularly slow in the fast lane, anger or frustration is a normal reaction. If a computer meltdown results in the loss of weeks of work, intense frustration and anger would be among the many natural reactions to this situation; others include feeling afraid, stressed, and overwhelmed. If being treated with fairness and respect is an important goal of yours, you might feel angry when you perceive mistreatment, unfairness, or rudeness toward you or others.

Unpleasant sensations and physical and emotional pain can also set off anger. Anger and hostility often go along for the ride with chronic pain. This makes a lot of sense when you think about it. We'd all like to be pain-free most of the time. When you feel chronic, sometimes debilitating pain, the resulting barriers to daily activities and the constant discomfort can be incredibly frustrating.

It is important to remember that different things make different people angry. Emotions such as anger involve very individual, personal experiences. Some people are really bothered by daily frustrations, such as being inconvenienced, whereas others take these events in stride. How you react emotionally to different situations depends on many factors, including personality and temperament; life experiences; the quality of diet and sleep; and whether you use alcohol, illegal drugs, or prescribed medication. The list goes on.

One of the first skills you'll learn in this book (chapter 4) is how to recognize the cues that tend to bring about anger for you. Being more aware of these cues and the overall patterns of your anger is the first step in learning how to manage anger.

UNDERSTANDING THE DIFFERENT COMPONENTS OF ANGER

An emotion is like a flower with many petals, although sometimes you might feel like your anger is the mythical, six-headed, snakelike Hydra! All emotions are made up of three different components: physical (the way your body responds when you experience an emotion), cognitive (the thoughts that go along with the emotion), and behavioral (the things you do or have urges to do when you experience an emotion).

Physical. Often the first tip-off that an emotion is occurring is a change in physical sensations. Some emotions, such as sadness, feel deflating and de-energizing. When you're sad, your limbs might feel heavy, you might have a sinking feeling in your chest or abdomen, and you might feel listless or lethargic. Things kind of slow down. In contrast, when you feel intensely afraid you might feel a lot more revved up and energized, and you might notice increased respiration, heavy and quick heartbeats, and perspiration.

Like fear, anger also tends to be an energizing emotion that comes with distinct and sometimes unpleasant physical sensations. What's interesting about these sensations is that they might be telling you that your body is preparing for action. Anger is one part of your body's natural defense system, often referred to as your flight-fight-freeze response. Anger is like a very sophisticated alarm system that alerts you to danger and prepares your body to take action. A lot of the physical sensations that go along with anger or fear involve changes in blood flow, which enable us to use our arms and legs more effectively to either flee quickly or defend ourselves. Changes in blood flow can cause increased heart rate, perspiration, narrowing of vision (in order to focus attention on a threat), muscle tension, increased sensitivity in hearing, racing thoughts, increased respiration, and dry mouth.

Imagine someone trying to break into a car of the future with this type of alarm system. First, the computer would perceive or sense that a person is touching the door handle. An alarm would go off, and the car would start. Then the flow of gas would increase, and the engine would rev higher and higher. The car would be completely ready to speed away from the intruder. When our alarm systems go off, our body is similarly preparing itself to quickly take action. Often the highest priority is to get away from the danger (flight); this is a common behavioral response to fear. With anger, however, another common reaction is essentially to fight—move toward, through, or around whatever is in our way. This reaction is why anger often goes hand in hand with the desire to act aggressively. There are many common physical sensations that accompany anger:

- Increased perspiration

- Increased heart rate

- Pounding heart

- Increased respiration

- Tense muscles

- Clenching or tightening in the chest

- Tightness in the jaw

- Dry mouth

- Feeling like things are not real

- Flushing of the face

- Feeling like you're going to explode

- Activation of flight-fight-freeze response

If you get used to noticing these physical signs of anger, you're one step closer to being able to identify and manage it more effectively. Many people have found that if they can identify bodily signs of anger before the signs get really intense, they can take action to avoid doing or saying things they later regret. We review many strategies for action in later chapters.

Another major component of any emotion, including anger, is a desire or urge to take action. In DBT language, we refer to this desire as an *action urge* (Linehan 1993b, 2015). As we already noted, many scientists think that one of the reasons emotions evolved in the first place was to prepare us to take action. When a large tiger saunters into your village, fear can prepare you to take action to protect yourself and loved ones. When someone says terrible things about you to other people, fear and indignation can motivate you to fix the situation and save your reputation.

Generally speaking, emotions usually come with action urges that involve the desire to move either toward or away from something. When anger makes you feel like moving toward something, you might feel like talking with or confronting the person you're angry with, moving or driving faster, or getting things out of your way. When anger makes you feel like moving away from things, you might feel like avoiding or distancing yourself from others, which can be self-protective actions if doing so prevents further harm. There are many common action urges that accompany anger:

- To be aggressive or violent

- To harm someone or something

- To keep going

- To talk quickly

- To seek revenge

- To make things hard for someone else

- To prove someone else wrong

- To voice your opinion

- To confront somebody

- To set things right

- To express how upset you are

- To get where you are going more quickly

When you feel angry, other physical changes occur that you don't even notice. Several areas in the brain are involved in emotions. When an emotional state occurs, activity occurs in a structure of the brain called the *amygdala*. The amygdala can be thought of as your brain's emotional engine. The hypothalamus, adrenal cortex, and pituitary gland also are involved in anger and stress responses. For example, the adrenal gland produces the stress hormone cortisol as a way to help your body adapt physically to stress. Over the long term, however, elevated cortisol levels can be damaging to your body.

Cognitive. The cognitive component of an emotion has to do with what and how you think when you're experiencing the emotion. Emotions are often accompanied by a number of different thoughts. When you are sad you might notice that you have sad thoughts, whereas when you're anxious you might notice that you experience a lot of worrisome thoughts. Anger is the same. Feelings of anger generally go hand in hand with specific types of thoughts and thinking patterns.

One very common thinking pattern that accompanies anger is called *rumination*. Rumination involves thinking over and over about something you don't like and wondering why it is happening or has happened (Nolen-Hoeksema 1991). Most of us are no strangers to rumination. For example, when stuck in traffic we might repeatedly think about how bad the traffic is, wonder why the person in front of us is going so slowly, mentally chastise ourselves for taking this particular route, and so on.

Rumination amplifies anger, making us more upset and making our problems seem more intolerable. When you're angry, the wheels are already spinning and the car is moving; rumination is like pressing even harder on the gas. In chapter 9 we discuss strategies to overcome and let go of rumination.

An important point to remember is that there's a back-and-forth relationship between thoughts and anger. Sometimes angry thoughts set off your anger. If the barista gets your drink wrong at a coffee shop, and you think to yourself, *What an incompetent jerk!* you're likely to feel angry. On the other hand, if you think to yourself, *Everyone makes mistakes. Maybe it's her first day on the job*, you might not feel as angry. At other times, you might feel really angry first, and as a result you start having angry thoughts—anger feeds angry thoughts and vice versa. Many common thoughts accompany anger:

- This person (or situation) is unfair.

- These people should not be doing what they are doing.

- I hate that person (or thing).

- This person (or situation) is bad or wrong.

- This person is being inconsiderate (or rude).

- This should not be happening.

- Someone (or something) is preventing me from doing what I want.

- This person is threatening my well-being (or that of someone close to me).

- I am to blame (in the case of anger directed toward yourself).

- This person (or group of people) is to blame.

- This is a catastrophe.

Behavioral. The third component of an emotion has to do with our actions. One common action is to express an emotion. This encompasses how we communicate what we are feeling through body language, facial expressions, words, or actions. Communicating emotions to other people has many benefits. When you express your emotions to people, they get to know you better and learn about your wants, needs, desires, likes, dislikes, and preferences. In this way, expressing emotions can bring you closer to others. You can probably imagine what it would be like to be in a relationship with someone who never expresses any emotion whatsoever. It would be very hard to get to know or feel close to such a person. Expressing emotions is part and parcel of why we experience them. In fact, one reason emotions have action urges associated with them is because emotions want to be expressed. This doesn't mean that it's good for our relationships if we yell and scream and do whatever else we feel like doing when we feel angry.

Probably you are reading this book because anger negatively affects your relationships. It's important to remember that most of the time, it's not the feelings of anger that cause problems in relationships but the ways people express them. Expressing anger can actually make relationships stronger. It is very important to learn how to convey anger in a way that helps rather than harms your relationships. Effectively expressing anger is much easier said than done, but in chapter 11 we discuss ways to do so.

People express anger verbally, through facial expressions, and through body language:

Verbal

- Yelling and screaming

- Threatening

- Criticizing

- Sarcasm

- Repeating oneself

- Complaining

- Mocking or mimicking

- Voicing one's opinion

- Monotone or flat voice

- Overly slow, punctuated, deliberate speech

Facial Expressions

- Scowling

- Frowning

- Eyebrows slanted downward

- Lips pursed or tight

- Eyes squinting or glaring

- Staring

- Grimacing

- Looking away

Body Language

- Rigid, tight hand gestures

- Moving around quickly

- Pacing

- Exaggerated gestures

- Rude gestures

- Being very still or quiet

- Stiff body movements

Just as there is a back-and-forth relationship between thoughts and anger, there is a back-and-forth relationship between behavior and anger. Anger can bring on angry behavior, and angry behavior can lead to more anger. Several years ago, some researchers performed an experiment to test this notion. They had one group of people punch a punching bag while thinking of a person who had angered them, while they directed another group to think of physical fitness as they punched the bag (Bushman 2002). Who do you think felt angrier afterward? Do you think it's a good idea to do whatever you need to do to get your anger out—to blow up and have an emotional release? If so, you might think that the people who punched the bag and thought of the person who angered them felt less angry. In fact, these were the folks who felt most angry and acted more aggressively later on when given the option to administer loud blasts of noise at the person who had angered them. (The experiment did not actually involve harming anyone; the subjects only thought they were administering noise at someone.) Thinking of the target of your anger while acting aggressively seems to increase anger and aggression.

Moving Forward

We hope that you have learned a few new things about anger from this overview. If so, you're already one step closer to learning how to deal effectively with your anger. If you practice the strategies in the following chapters, we are confident that you will start to notice important changes in your life. Anger can be a strong ally if you understand it, learn from it, know how to manage it, and use it effectively. We intend to help you do all of these things.

CHAPTER 2

Overview of DBT and DBT Skills

Having read chapter 1, you should have a better sense of what anger is and know more about what you're dealing with. This chapter provides an overview of DBT skills and explains why they can be so helpful for managing anger. Think of this chapter as the foundation for the rest of the book, in which you'll learn how to use the skills.

WHAT IS DBT?

Dialectical behavioral therapy is a type of psychological therapy developed by Dr. Marsha Linehan, a professor and psychologist at the University of Washington. Back in the late 1970s and early 1980s, Dr. Linehan was working with patients who were experiencing such intense emotional misery that they had tried to end their lives. She wanted to help them gain freedom from their misery and build fulfilling, happy lives. At the time, the best treatment available was cognitive behavioral therapy (CBT). CBT involves helping patients learn how to think differently about their lives, themselves, and their problems; learn new coping skills; and work toward concrete life goals, such as improving relationships, managing stress, getting a job, and improving health and fitness.

Though this type of treatment was considered very effective, Dr. Linehan had limited success with her patients who were experiencing intense and overwhelming misery. CBT almost completely focuses on helping people *change* their thoughts, feelings, and behavior, but trying to change thoughts, feelings, and behavior when you're suffering intensely is a lot like trying to relax or think positive thoughts while your foot is on fire.

Perhaps you can relate to this conundrum regarding your anger. Have you ever been really angry and had somebody suggest that you change your mind about the anger-inducing situation or that you use coping skills? If so, you probably know what we're talking about. You probably felt like the other person didn't really understand how you were feeling. Also, you were probably too upset to take any of this person's advice. When emotions are intense, changing thoughts and behaviors in the heat of the moment is very difficult.

Dr. Linehan came to realize that CBT was missing methods to help clients learn how to *accept* themselves, their emotions, their thoughts, and their life situations. People who are experiencing emotional turmoil often need to accept these things before they're really able to make important changes. In the same way, if anger is getting in the way of your life, you need to learn to accept that you have anger problems before you can do anything about them. To address this, DBT includes strategies that help clients balance acceptance and change.

WHAT DOES "DIALECTICAL" MEAN?

The need for both acceptance and change is where the "dialectical" part of DBT comes into play. A *dialectic* is the tension between two opposing forces, arguments, positions, or ideas. Perhaps you've heard of "thesis" (argument) and "antithesis" (counterargument). There's a saying that for every thesis there is an equally valid antithesis; basically, for anything you believe there is an equally valid opposite belief. For example, you might think *This rain is horrible and miserable* (thesis), and it might well be so. However, plenty of people appreciate the rain because it nourishes plants, trees, and grass and shores up the reservoir so people can have clean drinking water (antithesis). Thinking dialectically means seeing the truth in opposing ideas or sides. In DBT, the two opposing sides are acceptance and change.

Now let's think about acceptance and change in terms of anger. You're probably aware that you have problems with anger. To some extent, you've probably accepted that your anger is getting in the way of your life's goals. This acceptance is great news; it is a huge step. Many people find it very difficult to accept and acknowledge that they have anger problems. When they do accept this difficult truth, however, they are much more able to do something about it. Acceptance opens the door to change. If you refused to accept that you had anger problems or ignored them, you would probably never do anything about them. Anger would continue getting in your way.

Simply accepting that you have problems with anger, however, does not mean that you know what to do about them. Acceptance alone is probably not enough, particularly if you've been dealing with anger for a long time. You also need change in the form of practical advice, guidance, and coping skills to help you understand and manage your anger. You need both acceptance and change.

Besides offering a new way of thinking (thesis and antithesis), DBT is a good fit for anger management because many of its skills are designed to help you better understand and manage emotions. Whether you're dealing with anger, sadness, shame, anxiety, or some other emotion, DBT includes practical skills to help you tolerate emotions without acting on them, understand and label emotions, and reduce painful emotions. As you know, anger is an emotion that often leads people astray, mainly because it is so hard to resist urges to act on anger. DBT skills can help you avoid acting on impulse and instead do something wise— even when your anger is strong or overwhelming.

DBT includes four sets of skills: mindfulness, distress tolerance, interpersonal effectiveness, and emotion regulation. The next several sections describe these skills in a general manner, and the remaining chapters of this book discuss how to use them to manage different aspects of anger.

MINDFULNESS SKILLS

Mindfulness skills involve learning to pay attention to what you are experiencing right here, right now (Kabat-Zinn 1990; Linehan 1993a, 1993b, 2015; Nhat Hanh 1991). Some clients have expressed concerns about mindfulness, thinking that it is meditation or is related to a religion or spiritual practice. Rest assured, you don't need to sit and meditate for hours to learn mindfulness skills, nor do you need to practice a particular religion. Mindfulness is about being in the present moment and being aware of what is happening in the moment. Many of our clients, including those who struggle with anger, have found mindfulness skills to be life changing. We hope you have a similar experience.

There are six DBT mindfulness skills:

- **Mindfully attending to your experiences.** Pay close attention to something you're experiencing in the moment without struggling with it or trying to change it. You can mindfully attend to anything, from physical sensations to thoughts and emotions.

- **Objectively labeling your experiences.** Describe your experiences in an objective way (Linehan 1993b, 2015). If you were on a walk and wanted to objectively label your experience, you might say to yourself, *The birds are flying from tree to tree. I hear chirping. The clouds look white and billowy.* Simply describe the facts without judgments, inferences, opinions, guesses, or hunches. Don't assume anything. Be really concrete and specific, and stick to the facts.

- **Immersing yourself in the present activity.** Throw your mind and body into whatever you're doing in the present moment and pay attention to what you're experiencing (Linehan 1993b, 2015).

- **Do one thing at a time.** Focus all of your attention on one activity at a time rather than multitasking.

- **Avoid judging.** Let go of judgments and evaluations. Rather than evaluating or judging something as good or bad or right or wrong, simply describe things exactly as they are (Linehan 1993b, 2015).

- **Do what works.** Rather than beating your head against the wall doing things that you want to do or feel like doing but ultimately don't work, learn from your experiences and do the things that help you reach your goals (Linehan 1993b, 2015).

Mindfulness skills can help you with anger in many ways. They can help you notice your anger earlier, before it becomes really intense. They can help you become more aware of the situations or experiences that make you angry. They can also be the antidote to the thinking patterns that accompany anger and tend to fan its flames.

DISTRESS TOLERANCE SKILLS

Distress tolerance skills are designed to help you get through really difficult or anger-provoking situations without making them worse. There are two types: *Crisis survival skills* involve learning to ride out an overwhelming situation until you can do something about it. *Reality acceptance skills* help you reduce misery and suffering by acknowledging and accepting things as they are (Linehan 1993b, 2015).

Crisis Survival Skills

One of the biggest problems with anger is that many of the action urges that go along with it are destructive. If you act on them, you can easily make things worse. Learning how to avoid acting on these urges is one of the most effective ways to manage anger. Crisis survival skills (reviewed in chapters 7 and 8) are designed to help you get through a very difficult situation without making things worse:

- Leaving the situation

- Distracting yourself with activities or strong sensations

- Self-soothing to calm your mind and body

- Thinking through the advantages of not acting on angry impulses and the disadvantages of acting on them

- Breathing and muscle relaxation

- Changing your body temperature

- Releasing the energy related to anger, such as through intense physical activity

Reality Acceptance Skills

Reality acceptance skills can help you reduce misery and suffering by acknowledging and accepting things as they are. When people feel angry, they often don't want to accept the way things are. Anger usually propels us to take action to change whatever is making us angry: get obstacles out of our way, communicate our opinions or feelings, and so on. This is fine if what's making you angry can be fixed in the moment, but life is often not like that.

Refusing to accept whatever is making you angry can just make your anger worse. If someone says something upsetting to you and you get caught up in resentment, refuse to accept that it happened, and ruminate, you're probably going to feel even more angry. If you deny or pretend that nothing was said, you probably won't do anything about it, such as talk it through with the person. On the other hand, if you accept and acknowledge that this person said something upsetting, you might be more likely to do something to make the situation better for yourself. Although we do not directly cover reality acceptance skills in later chapters, you might find it useful to practice accepting your anger and the cues for your anger as you work on other skills in this book. For further reading about reality acceptance, please see *DBT Skills Training Manual*, second edition (Linehan 2015), and *Radical Acceptance* (Brach 2003).

INTERPERSONAL EFFECTIVENESS SKILLS

Often the greatest feelings of joy, misery, disappointment, excitement, and anger occur in the context of our relationships. And people with anger problems often have difficulty interacting with other people.

One of the most effective ways to manage anger is to express it. If you listen carefully, anger can tell you something about what you want or need. And if you express anger in a healthy and respectful way, it often diminishes. What's more, you might actually get your needs met or solve the problem that made you angry in the first place.

If you've found that expressing anger hasn't worked for you in the past, or if it has made things worse, the idea that expressing anger can be helpful might be surprising. The good news is that interpersonal effectiveness skills can help you express anger in a way that other people may be willing to hear. These skills focus on two main things (Linehan 2015):

- **Identifying your goals.** When it comes to expressing anger, you're going to want to figure out what it's telling you. What exactly do you want the other person to do or say? You might want that person to treat you more kindly, ask you about your day, clean up more around the house, or recognize the work you do. Identifying your goals is a lot like having a clear idea of where you want to go before you set out on a journey. By doing so, you're much more likely to get to your destination. Similarly, figuring out ahead of time what you want and need from another person can make it much more likely that you will have your needs met.

- **Learning how to express your anger and needs effectively.** In chapter 11 we discuss using nonjudgmental language; objectively labeling your experiences; using nonaggressive words, voice tone, and body language; and developing a script for what you want to say and practicing the script ahead of time. By implementing these strategies, you can improve your interactions with other people, manage and resolve conflict, and express your anger in a way that works well for you and your relationships. And by practicing them, you might also improve your social support, feel better about your life, and develop fulfilling and meaningful relationships, all of which can help you maintain whatever progress you have made with your anger-related problems.

EMOTION REGULATION SKILLS

If you're struggling with anger, emotion regulation skills might be what you need most. Emotion regulation involves the ways people influence which emotions they have, when they have them, and how they experience and express them (Gross 1998). Emotion regulation skills help you manage emotions in three primary ways.

First, there are skills that help you learn how to identify and understand your emotions (Linehan 1993b, 2015) so they feel more manageable and less distressing and frightening. In chapter 4 we provide guidance on how to recognize cues for anger, identify and recognize the three components of anger (physical, cognitive, and behavioral), keep track of and learn about your own patterns of anger, and recognize anger in the moment.

Second, there are skills to help you reduce your vulnerability to intense emotions, including anger. In chapter 5 we go over ways to improve your physical and emotional self-care, engage in positive activities, and do things that make you feel confident and capable (Linehan 1993b, 2015).

Third, there are skills to help you manage your emotions and reduce the intensity of anger. In chapter 6 we discuss how you can step back, notice, and pay attention to your emotions without escaping or struggling with them. In chapter 10 we discuss how you can do the opposite of what you feel like doing when you experience an emotion (Linehan 1993b, 2015).

Moving Forward

We hope you have a better understanding of what anger is and how the skills in this book will help you manage it more effectively. To review, Dr. Marsha Linehan developed DBT as a treatment for people suffering from intense and complex emotions. The main idea of this treatment is that balancing self-acceptance with coping skills and other strategies is the best way to change and solve the problems causing intense emotions. DBT includes four main sets of skills, each of which can help with anger: mindfulness, distress tolerance, interpersonal effectiveness, and emotion regulation. Throughout the rest of this book we review the skills from each of these areas that are most applicable to anger. In the next chapter, we'll help you figure out how to get and stay motivated to work on your anger.

CHAPTER 3

Getting and Staying Motivated to Work on Your Anger

Motivation can be a powerful force behind the major changes we make in life. Once you've decided that you really want to change how you deal with anger, you're likely to take steps to work on it. Strong motivation is especially important when you are trying to make difficult changes. When changing long-standing behavior you really need extra fuel to keep going. It can be very difficult to change angry behavior, so motivation is important.

It may seem odd to devote a whole chapter to ways you can motivate yourself to work on anger. After all, you've already taken the step of purchasing this book. Aren't you already motivated enough? You might be, but there are a few important things you need to know about motivation.

THINGS THAT INFLUENCE MOTIVATION

First, what do we mean by "motivation"? Motivation is your drive or desire to do something, such as change behavior, reduce angry outbursts, change life circumstances, and so on. Desires, however, change a lot depending on many factors, including your life situation, your emotional state, your mood, the emotions you're experiencing, the level of stress in your life, and how well you're taking care of yourself. Even something as basic to human survival as the motivation to eat can change. For example, if you haven't eaten for a while, you're probably going to feel hungry, and this hunger might motivate you to find something to eat. If you just ate a large meal, however, and someone asks you out for lunch, you might feel less motivated to go out and eat. If you are hungry but then hear tragic news about a close relative, you might completely lose interest in eating for a short period of time.

Similarly, your motivation to change how you manage your anger might also fluctuate. If you recently experienced a rough period in which your anger got in the way of your relationships, you might feel more motivated to change. When things have been going smoothly, it's common to have less motivation. You might think to yourself, *Nothing's really wrong, so why work on changing?* At times you might be so emotionally or physically exhausted from all of the other things you're doing that tackling anger is the last thing you want to do. The bottom line is that motivation waxes and wanes. So even if you start off with a ton of motivation to manage your anger, there will come a time when your motivation is reduced. At these times you can rely on the skills in this chapter. They'll become your best friend when it's hard to get and sustain motivation.

AMBIVALENCE ABOUT CHANGE IS THE RULE, NOT THE EXCEPTION

Another important thing to know is that there will be times when you want to change and don't want to change at the same time. This is called "ambivalence." There are probably things about your anger that you like or don't feel like you should have to change. At times it might seem like other people are the problem. If they would just stop being so annoying, or stop being so sensitive, or become better drivers, you wouldn't be so angry. So why should you have to change? At the same time, you might consider all of the reasons why your life would be better if you could free yourself from anger.

It can be hard to sustain motivation when you want to change and don't want to change at the same time. The good news is that researchers have been working for decades on skills to help people deal with ambivalence.

YOUR MOTIVATION MIGHT NEED A BOOST

When learning to deal with something as challenging as anger, sometimes you need a boost in motivation to keep going. Trying to understand and manage an emotion such as anger can be a lot like riding a restless racehorse. Both take determination, discipline, and hard work. If understanding and managing anger were easy, you probably wouldn't need this book. In fact, we think anger is one of the most difficult emotions to manage, because unlike some other emotions, anger pushes you to take action. To effectively manage anger, you not only have to understand and learn how to cope with it, but you also have to learn *impulse control*—how to stop yourself from doing things that might cause trouble, such as having angry outbursts. Because managing anger is such a difficult task, you need the extra fuel that strong motivation provides to keep yourself doing the hard work when it becomes difficult. With the help of the skills in this book, we are confident you can stay motivated.

HOW MOTIVATED ARE YOU TO WORK ON ANGER?

Years ago, a couple of psychologists (Prochaska and DiClemente 1984) proposed a helpful way to think about motivation in the context of making changes in one's life. Their work focused mostly on changing drinking behavior, but the model they developed is useful for any behavior. The *transtheoretical model of change* says that people go through different stages on their way to changing behavior.

Precontemplation

During the *precontemplation stage*, people aren't even thinking about changing their behavior. For example, a smoker who hasn't seriously considered quitting would be at this stage. If you are in this stage with anger, it means you don't recognize or understand that you have a problem with anger, nor have you given any thought to working on it. If someone suggested that you learn coping skills to deal with anger, you might be surprised (and perhaps a little angry) and ask why. The fact that you are reading this book probably means you are past the precontemplation stage, unless you picked up this book because you are trying to understand the struggles of someone else in your life. Just buying this book means you are already considering changing your behavior.

People who are in this first stage would agree with most of these statements about anger:

- I haven't given much thought to doing anything about my anger.

- I don't think I have a problem with anger.

- Other people might think I have a problem, but they're the ones who need to change.

- It's normal to feel anger as often or as intensely as I do.

- I don't think it's a problem to yell from time to time.

- Other people probably feel as angry as I do.

- There aren't any downsides to my anger.

Contemplation

In the *contemplation stage*, people are starting to think about changing their behavior. If you're in this stage, you might have noticed that anger is affecting your relationships or your job. Maybe you recognize that even though anger has benefits, it also has downsides. Perhaps your anger is so intense or frequent that your health is at risk or you feel tense and stressed a lot of the time. Or maybe the things you do when you feel angry, such as yelling at or threatening those who are close to you, are causing problems for you. By the time you're thinking about changing how you manage anger, you've probably begun to notice some of its costs.

• Sandy's Story

Sandy first realized that she needed to work on her anger at a family gathering in a restaurant. At the table one of her relatives was complaining about the food and scowling and snapping at his wife. Sandy could feel anger and frustration bubbling up inside her. She recognized how upset she was, so she tried to distract herself by talking with others at the table. But eventually she couldn't contain her anger. She blew up and told her relative that he was acting like a child and should leave. Not only did this occur in front of everyone at the table, but others in the restaurant looked over to see what was happening. Afterward, she felt incredibly guilty and embarrassed. Even before this event she knew that she had a problem; others had commented about her "hot temper." She knew that she felt irritable a lot, and she often would blow up in arguments with her partner. This event at dinner, however, tipped the scales and made her seriously consider getting help for her anger. She had entered the contemplation stage.

If you find yourself agreeing with most of the statements below, you're likely in the contemplation stage. If so, you are probably in touch with both the positives and negatives of your anger. The good news is that people who study and treat motivation think this is an excellent place to be. You're probably ready to take action and learn how to effectively manage anger.

- Others comment on my anger or my angry behavior.

- I find myself acting in ways that go against my values.

- I hurt other people's feelings when I am angry.

- I spend more time feeling angry than I'd like to.

- I feel more angry than I'd like to.

- I am not sure that my anger is normal.

- I think I have a problem with anger.

- I know that anger has benefits.

- I like some things about my anger.

Preparation

In the *preparation stage*, people are sure that something needs to change and are preparing to make changes. If you're in this stage, you've probably come to terms with the negative effects anger is having on your life, and you are starting to devise a plan to change the way you cope with anger. Among other things, this plan might involve gathering as much information about anger as you can, learning new coping skills, reading books like this one, or seeking professional help from a therapist or counselor. The key idea here is that you're willing to accept that you have a problem and need to do something about it.

If most of the statements below ring true, you're probably in the preparation stage. This is excellent news! You're poised and ready to make important changes in your life.

- I have started to read and learn about anger.

- I am thinking about the things I need to do to work on my anger.

- I made an appointment with a therapist or counselor.

- I spoke to or agreed with a loved one about the need to work on my anger.

- I made a list (either physically or mentally) of things I plan to do to work on my anger.

- I sought advice from someone about how to deal with my anger.

Taking Action Steps

The next stage is to take *action steps* to put your plan into action. You might read a book about managing your anger more effectively, practice new coping skills (such as those we discuss in this book), take a course or attend a group therapy session on anger management, surf the Internet for information about anger and anger management, or start seeing a therapist. You know you're in this stage if you've started trying to fix your anger problems.

Maintenance

People in the *maintenance stage* have done a lot of work on their anger and have made important changes. This is the final stage, in which all of the new skills you've learned come together to help you manage your anger more effectively. You might feel happier, more fulfilled—like anger is your ally, not your enemy.

Unsurprisingly, the main goal of the maintenance stage is to maintain the changes you've set in motion. This is not easy to do. As hard as it is to make changes in the first place, it can be even harder to maintain those changes. Think about smoking. Many people try quitting many times before they actually succeed. They serve as examples that maintaining a change in behavior can be challenging. As difficult as it can be to change behaviors for the long term, the skills in this book will help you do just that.

SKILLS TO BOOST YOUR MOTIVATION

Now that you have a better sense of your level of motivation to work on anger, it's time to figure out how to give your motivation a boost. The skills below come from DBT (Linehan 1993b, 2015) and other treatments that focus on improving motivation, such as motivational interviewing (Miller and Rollnick 2012). We focus on three primary ways to boost your motivation: considering the pros and cons of anger-related behavior, becoming more aware of the effect anger has on your life, and making a commitment to change.

Consider the Pros and Cons of Anger-Related Behavior

One of the best ways to boost motivation and tip the scales of ambivalence in favor of changing a behavior is to weigh the pros (positives, or benefits) and cons (negatives, or downsides) of a particular behavior (Linehan 1993b, 2015). We have found this skill to be very helpful for motivating people to change a variety of behaviors, including self-harm, drug and alcohol use, and angry outbursts. By thinking through the pros and cons of how you manage and deal with your anger, you'll get a better sense of both the advantages and problems related to your anger. Seeing the pros and cons together in one place and being able to compare them can give you information about whether the pros outweigh the cons.

Use exercise 3.1 to identify the pros and cons of how you currently manage anger. Think about how you generally manage anger, how anger affects your life, and how you express anger (the things you typically do when you're angry). Here are a few pointers for beginning this exercise:

- If you're having a lot of angry outbursts, such as yelling or being emotionally or physically aggressive, it might be a good idea to focus on these behaviors.

- If you feel angry a lot of the time but don't act out in anger, it might be a good idea to focus on the impact that chronic anger has on your life.

Once you've identified the pros and cons of how you manage anger, think through the pros and cons of working on your anger (Linehan 1993b, 2015). This might seem odd, as the whole book is focused on managing anger, but there are probably very good reasons why you haven't yet gotten a handle on your anger. One reason might be that working on anger is hard. Another might be that you have not yet accepted that you have a problem. Whatever your situation, getting a sense of both the downsides and upsides of working on anger can help you know what you're getting into, what might be difficult about it, and why you're doing it.

Exercise 3.1 Pros and Cons of Anger and Working on Anger

Angry Behavior	Pros	Cons
Example: *Yelling*	Pro: *It makes me feel strong and powerful.*	Con: *It is hurting my family and my relationships.*
Working on Anger	Pros	Cons
	Example: *I would feel better about myself.*	Example: *It is a lot of work, and I'm already busy enough.*

After you complete this exercise, circle the cons of anger-related behavior and the pros of working on your anger. Then put a star next to the examples that are most important or costly to you. If having a better relationship with your partner is the most important reason for working on your anger, then put a star next to it. If trouble maintaining a job is the most costly aspect of your anger, then put a star next to it. Memorize these important pros and cons so you can always remember why you're trying to deal with anger more effectively. These pros and cons will give you fuel to keep going when things are hard.

• Sam's Story

Sam got really angry and yelled and threw things at her partner, Ted, when he asked her whether she had started looking for a job. Sam had been out of work for about two months, and she and Ted were under financial strain. Part of the reason she was out of work was her anger. She had yelled at her boss and kicked his desk after he said that he couldn't give her a raise. When Ted brought up the job issue, she felt embarrassed, ashamed, and then angry all over again. Sam had just started therapy before the blowup with her partner. Afterward she took some time to think through the pros and cons of her angry outbursts. She entered the *pros of working on anger* and the *cons of angry outbursts* into the notes section of her smartphone. The next time Ted brought up the subject of her employment, Sam discreetly looked at her notes: *I love Ted, and I know he is stressed about money. I know he doesn't mean to annoy me. I don't want to hurt his feelings. If I keep yelling at him, things are going to go downhill fast. If I try to keep my anger in check, I will feel less guilty after we talk.* She took a deep breath, looked up at Ted, and told him how she felt ashamed, embarrassed, and angry when he brought up her job situation. She apologized for having yelled and thrown things at him the last time he brought it up, and they sat down and came up with a plan: they formalized a household budget and brainstormed a list of places for her to apply for a job.

Becoming Aware of the Effect Anger Has on Your Life

One of the best ways to increase your motivation to work on anger is to get in touch with the negative effects it has on your life. People often go through life without really thinking about how their behavior is bringing them closer to or pushing them further away from the kind of life they want. The good news is there are ways to become more aware of anger's negative effects.

Examine whether anger is getting in the way of what matters in your life. Think about the life you want to live, and then compare that to your current life (Miller and Rollnick 2012). For most people, there is a difference between the two. Perhaps you would like to have more fulfilling relationships, work less, spend more time with your family, have more fun, or be more physically fit or healthy. When people start to see how anger gets in the way of what's really important, they feel motivated to make changes.

In exercise 3.2, which follows, we list different areas of life that many people value, but we might be missing some that are important to you. If so, just add your own. Then follow these steps:

1. Think about your values and how they apply to the categories in the left-hand column of the table. Values have to do with what's important to you. For example, if it's important to you to be a loving parent, then you value being a loving parent.

2. Describe how you would like things to be in the middle column. For the "Relationships with Friends" value you might write, *I would like to feel closer to my friends* or *I would like to have more friends and see them more often.* Do this for each category.

3. Think about whether anger-related behaviors, such as angry outbursts or feeling angry a lot of the time, are getting in the way of your values. Rate this on a scale from 0 (anger is not getting in the way of my values) to 10 (anger is completely blocking me from my values) in the right-hand column.

Exercise 3.2   Does Anger Interfere with
Important Areas of Your Life?

Values	How You Would Like Things to Be	Does Anger Interfere with Your Values?
Relationships with friends		
Relationships with family		
Relationships with others		
Occupational/ job goals		
Financial goals		
Spiritual/ religious goals		
Recreational goals		
Fitness/health goals		
Other goals		

Values	How You Would Like Things to Be	Does Anger Interfere with Your Values?
Other goals		

Another way to get in touch with the negative effects that anger has on your life is to think about how things would be different if you coped with anger effectively. Consider what you do when you're angry and how things would be different if you stopped doing these things. How would your life change if you didn't yell at loved ones or didn't feel irritable all the time or didn't drive recklessly? In exercise 3.3 take some time to write about what your life would be like if you coped with anger effectively.

Exercise 3.3　What Your Life Would Be Like
If You Could Cope with Anger Effectively

Making a Commitment to Change

When dealing with anger or other difficulties, you might find yourself at a fork in the road. One path leads to more of the same (angry outbursts, relationship problems, trouble at work), whereas the other path leads to goals that are important to you. Making a commitment to change is like stepping squarely onto that second path—the one that will take you where you really want to go. By "want," we mean where your values and goals tell you to go. When you're angry, you might want to step onto the more destructive path, but in your wisest state of mind, when you're really in touch with your values, you will want to take the other path. There are several ways to increase your commitment.

Take action steps. Get moving in your work on anger (Miller and Rollnick 2012). Action steps might involve reading a book like this one; making an appointment with a therapist or counselor; talking with your partner, a friend, or a confidant about how you'd like to manage anger more effectively; or starting to keep track of your anger (see chapter 4). Making a commitment is not just wrestling your brain into submission and convincing yourself to work on anger; it can be the act of moving forward on that path toward your goals. Have you noticed how the first few pedal strokes on your bicycle get the wheels turning and the bike moving by its own momentum? The same thing can happen when you start taking action steps. Momentum can build, making it easier to keep going.

Talk about your commitment. Talk with others about your anger, acknowledge your problem, and publicly commit to change. Studies (Lokhorst et al. 2013) in social psychology research have found that people are much more likely to sustain public commitments (those made with other people or with others present) than private commitments (those you make with yourself). There are several ways to make your commitments more public:

- Talk with a close friend or loved one about the steps you're willing to take to better manage your anger.

- Make a specific agreement with someone that you will try out a coping skill (such as muscle relaxation or deep breathing, discussed in chapter 8) the next time you feel like blowing up.

- Tell someone that you bought this book and want to start working on your anger.

- Send an e-mail to a friend explaining changes you plan to make with your anger management.

- Make an agreement with your partner to use specific steps to express yourself in a less irritable manner the next time you feel annoyed.

- Commit to your therapist to do anger-management homework.

- Tell your therapy group how you plan to work on your anger between now and the next meeting.

- Make specific commitments each week with someone else who is working on anger.

If you decide to make public commitments, we have a few pointers:

- First, avoid committing to unrealistic goals. Don't tell someone that you'll never again lose your temper or that all of your anger-related problems will be gone in a month. Make reasonable and doable commitments.

- Second, commit to something specific. Although it's definitely okay to tell someone that you plan to "work on your anger," which is a general goal, it can be more effective to follow up with a more specific commitment, such as "by practicing deep-breathing skills twice this week."

- Third, make sure you are accountable for what you did or did not do. If you tell a friend that you will practice your breathing skills this week, make sure your friend follows up with you. If your friend doesn't check in with you, you might be less likely to continue practicing. Encourage your friends or loved ones to hold you accountable to your commitments. Therapists do this naturally, as they're trained to, but friends and family may need suggestion.

TIPS FOR GETTING STARTED

Now that you've learned some skills for boosting and maintaining your motivation, we have a couple of tips for getting started. You can also use these to work on other emotions, problems, or behaviors.

Start Small

Changing patterns in life, including how you manage anger, can be overwhelming. In fact, it can be so overwhelming that you don't even know where to begin. The answer is to start small.

Working on anger is a lot like moving to a new home. Moving can be a stressful life event. There are so many things to do: finding boxes, packing up your belongings, calling the movers, determining what to keep and what to get rid of, unpacking, getting the cable and phone connected, and on and on. Focusing on the big task of moving can be overwhelming. And when you're overwhelmed, you are more likely to avoid or procrastinate. The same thing can happen with anger. If you focus on the big task of managing anger more effectively, you might be so overwhelmed that you give up before you even begin.

It can be much more effective to focus on each small step in the process of working on anger. Start with the bigger picture, but then break it down into smaller steps. The idea is to have only one thing to do at a time. For example, if you don't want to throw things when you feel angry, break this goal into more manageable steps:

- Learn to recognize when you're angry so you know when you're at risk of blowing up and throwing things. Keep track of your patterns of anger (chapter 4). You could also get familiar with the types of situations that bring up anger and the times when you're most likely to throw things.

- Practice skills (chapter 7) that help you avoid acting impulsively when you're angry.

- Notice your urge or desire to throw things, and practice resisting the urge. You could start small by resisting other urges, such as the urge to eat chocolate or take the next sip of coffee. Then when you feel the urge to throw something, you could try the skills from chapter 7.

- Keep practicing the skills that work regularly until it becomes easier to resist the urge to throw things.

Now it's your turn. Come up with a goal regarding your anger and put together a few small, manageable steps you can focus on over the next week to help you attain the goal.

Exercise 3.4 Determine a Goal and Action Steps

Goal	
Step 1	
Step 2	
Step 3	
Other steps	

Encouraging and Rewarding Yourself

As you begin or continue to work on anger, it can be helpful to find ways to encourage yourself with what we call "cheerleading" statements in DBT (Linehan 1993a). Come up with things you can say to yourself that give you fuel to keep going, help you remember your strengths, and make you feel good about the progress you've made. The most effective cheerleading statements are ones that you believe:

- I can do this.
- I have been through worse before, so I know I can get through this.
- I have the strength to keep going.
- I am smart enough (or wise enough, capable enough) to do this.
- I did a really great job at ____________________.

Another way to encourage yourself is to remember that each step you take brings you closer to your goal. Even if you get really frustrated and turn around and start going back in the opposite direction, all is not lost. Any steps you have already taken can make it easier to get back on track again in the future. The process of changing your behavior is a lot like forging a new path in the forest. You might be used to walking down the same path repeatedly, and that path is probably well-worn and easy to traverse. Think of this as the problems-with-anger path. To turn things around, you have to start hacking away with a machete to create a new path. This process is hard at first, but even if you make only a little progress before turning around, the next time you return the new path will still be clearer than when you started.

Finally, don't forget to reward yourself for any progress you make, even the smallest of steps. If you successfully monitor your anger and fill out worksheet 4.1 (see chapter 4) three days in a row, do something nice for yourself. If you avoid a blowup at work by effectively using relaxation strategies or the skill of opposite action (see chapter 10), tell somebody about it—brag a little! Telling others about your success can elicit encouragement and praise, both of which can be very motivational. Notice the small changes that you make; don't discount them. It's important to give yourself credit for hard work and any progress you make. Exercise 3.5 can help you with this.

1. First, brainstorm ways that you might reward yourself for taking small but important steps in your work on anger. The rewards should be important to you—things you'd actually be willing to work for. We included examples to get you started, but it's really important to personalize this.

2. Next, think through and describe important steps you've already taken in your work on anger. You've already bought this book, and perhaps you've gotten through the first couple of chapters. Or maybe you made an appointment for a therapy session. Perhaps you're already practicing new anger-management skills, such as muscle relaxation or deep breathing. Whatever steps you've taken, acknowledge them by writing them down. Also, consider future steps that you plan to take.

Exercise 3.5   Plan Your Rewards and Acknowledge Important Steps

Rewards You Are Willing to Work For

Go to my favorite coffee shop for a drink I don't normally get.

Spend time playing my favorite game on my iPhone, computer, or gaming system.

Tell somebody (brag) about important steps I've taken.

_____

_____

_____

Important Steps You Have Taken

Read through a few chapters of the anger workbook.

Told my partner I would work on my angry outbursts.

Started practicing deep breathing.

_____

_____

_____

Moving Forward

In this chapter, we focused on ways to boost and maintain the motivation to change angry behavior. Motivation is your desire, interest, or intention to change, and strategies to keep up or boost your motivation can be invaluable. These strategies include getting in touch with the effect anger has on your life, noting progress toward important goals, and making a firm commitment to change. As you work on anger, remember that it can be helpful to start with small, realistic steps and goals and to use encouragement and rewards to keep yourself going. In chapter 4 we discuss ways to help you understand your own patterns of anger, because understanding these patterns puts you in a better position to anticipate and cope with anger.

CHAPTER 4

Understanding Your Own Patterns of Anger

When it comes to managing anger, the first step is actually to understand your anger. We realize that this may seem counterintuitive. You may think the best way to manage your anger is to avoid it whenever possible—to try to not be in touch with your anger so you aren't at risk of acting on it. The problem with this is that trying to manage your anger by avoiding it is a lot like trying to find your way around a new city without a map. If you have no idea how the streets are laid out, getting from one place to another without getting lost is very difficult. The same is true for your anger. It's going to be a lot more difficult to navigate your anger if you don't know all of its nooks and crannies and twists and turns. Therefore, the first step in managing your anger is to get in touch with it and understand all aspects of it. This includes understanding the types of situations and experiences that tend to bring up anger for you—or the cues for your anger—as well as understanding your own personal experience of anger.

IDENTIFYING THE CUES FOR YOUR ANGER

Although there are probably times when it feels like your anger comes out of the blue, all emotions are cued by something. That's the way emotions work. Even if you aren't able to figure out what cued your anger in any given moment, rest assured that something did. And knowing what tends to cue your anger will make you better prepared to manage it.

When identifying the cues for your anger, it's important to describe these cues in a particular way. The DBT skill of objectively labeling your experience (Linehan 1993b, 2015) allows you to describe these cues in the most helpful way. The point of this skill is to describe your experiences in a neutral, matter-of-fact way by just sticking to the facts. Rather than judging or evaluating the situations or experiences that bring up anger for you (which will probably only add fuel to the fire and make you more angry!), simply describe these experiences exactly as they are. For example, let's say that your father said something that angered you. Describing the situation objectively would mean describing exactly what happened and what he said. Instead of saying "He was rude" or "He was a jerk," you'd say, "My dad called me this morning and told me that he doesn't approve of my job and thinks I should do something else." Separate your evaluations ("rude") and judgments ("jerk") from the facts (what your father actually said and did). Not only will this skill help you identify the specific cues for your anger so you can address them head-on, it will keep you from adding fuel to the fire and fanning the flames of your anger as you think about these cues.

You may notice that evaluations and judgments continue to pop into your head from time to time, especially when you first start practicing this skill. This is natural and to be expected. If this happens, simply notice the evaluation or judgment and bring your attention back to describing the experience objectively. The goal of this skill is not to get rid of judgments and evaluations completely, which would be impossible, but to avoid getting caught up in them as much.

As we discussed in chapter 1, there are many different types of experiences and situations that elicit feelings of anger. Although some of the most common cues for anger involve someone or something threatening your well-being (or the well-being of someone you care about) or blocking you from something you want, these cues can take a number of different forms. Therefore, it's important to figure out what brings up anger for you. Exercise 4.1 can help you with this.

Exercise 4.1   Identifying Your Cues for Anger

Close your eyes and take a few minutes to think about the types of situations and experiences that tend to bring up anger for you. What situations, events, people, or objects tend to cue your anger? Think about times you experienced anger recently and what was going on at that time.

The following list contains common cues for anger. Mark all that apply to you.

☐ Waiting in line

☐ Not getting what you want

☐ Having someone disagree with you

☐ Being cut off while driving

☐ Being told no

☐ Driving in traffic

☐ Being insulted

☐ Being attacked

☐ Chronic pain

☐ Being prevented from doing something you want to do

☐ Not having your opinions or wishes taken into account

☐ Calling customer service

☐ Being overcharged

☐ Observing people mistreating animals, children, or other adults

Are there other situations that tend to bring up feelings of anger? Please list them below.

1. _____

2. _____

3. _____

4. _____

5. _____

6. _____

7. _____

Knowing the types of situations and experiences that tend to bring up feelings of anger is an important first step in learning to manage your anger. One of the things that can make anger so overwhelming is the sense that it comes out of the blue. Anything that's unpredictable, whether it's an emotion, a thought, or a stressful situation, tends to be a lot more difficult to manage than something we can predict. Therefore, the better you become at pinpointing the situations and experiences that bring up anger for you, the more manageable your anger will be. Becoming more aware of your personal anger cues will also allow you to plan ahead and use some of the other skills in this book.

RECOGNIZING AND IDENTIFYING ANGER

As helpful as it can be to know the situations and experiences that tend to make you angry, this is only the first step in understanding your anger. As you may remember from chapter 1, all emotions are made up of three components: physical (the way your body responds when you experience an emotion), cognitive (the thoughts that go along with the emotion), and behavioral (the things you do or have urges to do when you experience an emotion). Identifying the different components of your anger and becoming more aware of each one will make it easier to recognize your anger sooner (Linehan 1993b).

You may find this surprising, but many people who struggle with anger are not very aware of their anger. Although they may be aware of their anger when it is really intense, they often have difficulty recognizing less intense feelings of anger. The downside of this is that less intense anger is easier to manage. Skills that are helpful when anger is a 3 or a 4 on a scale from 0 to 10 don't always work as well when anger is an 8 or 9. It's just more difficult to cope with intense anger. That's why it's important to learn how to recognize your anger when it is less intense. Doing so will give you many more options for managing your anger and expressing it effectively.

Mindfully Attending to Your Experience Without Judging It

The DBT skill of mindfully attending to your experience without judging it (Linehan 1993b) will help you become more aware of your anger and how it feels in your body. Rather than getting swept up in your anger or reacting to it, the goal of this skill is to just notice all of the different parts of your emotion without pushing them away or clinging to them. The first part of this skill involves simply paying attention to the physical sensations, thoughts, and action urges that go along with anger, watching each of these experiences arise and pass from one moment to the next. To start, it may be helpful to bring your attention to how the anger feels in your body and the different sensations you're experiencing. Then bring your attention to the thoughts that are present and any urges you're experiencing to act in some way. If you find yourself getting caught up in your thoughts or desires to act in a certain way, gently turn your attention back to how the emotion feels in your body.

The second part of this skill involves *how* to go about observing the different components of your anger. As you notice each component of your emotion, be sure to take an objective and neutral stance. Focus on just noticing each sensation, thought, or urge as it is (for example, a feeling of tension here, a feeling of heat or warmth there, the thought *This isn't fair*, or an urge to yell), rather than judging it as bad or wrong. Keep in mind that anger is a natural part of being alive. It's something that every human being experiences. Observing your anger in an objective way will help you learn that it is not inherently dangerous or problematic. This skill will also help you become more aware of and accepting of your anger.

One way to begin practicing this skill is to think about a recent time when you felt anger. Not only will this give you a chance to practice this skill at any time, even if you aren't currently feeling angry, it will also allow you to begin practicing this skill on anger that isn't too intense. You can choose the experience of anger you want to focus on and practice this skill initially on anger that feels more manageable. Exercise 4.2 provides simple step-by-step instructions for mindfully attending to the components of your anger without judgment.

Exercise 4.2   Mindfully Attending to Your Anger

1. Find a comfortable and quiet place where you can sit or lie down.

2. Close your eyes.

3. Focus on your breathing. Notice what it feels like to breathe in and breathe out. Notice which parts of your body move as you breathe in and out.

4. Think about a recent time when you felt anger at a moderate level of intensity. Try to focus on a time when your anger was around a 4 or 5 on a scale from 0 to 10, where 0 equals no emotion and 10 equals the most intense emotion possible. Focus on this experience and try to get a clear picture of it in your mind.

5. Bring your attention to your body and notice where in your body you feel the emotion. Scan your body from head to toe, paying attention to any sensations in your head, neck, shoulders, back, chest, abdomen, arms, hands, legs, and feet. Spend about ten seconds on each area of your body, stepping back in your mind and just paying attention to and noticing the sensations.

6. Once you have finished scanning your body, bring your attention to the parts of your body where you feel anger. Zero in on these sensations. Watch them rise and fall in your mind's eye as you would watch a wave do so on the ocean.

7. If you begin to label or judge the sensations, notice that evaluation or judgment, and then bring your attention back to noticing the sensations as just sensations.

8. Bring your attention to any thoughts that are present, focusing on just noticing these thoughts as thoughts without attaching to them. If you find yourself getting caught up in your thoughts or judging yourself for having them, notice that and then bring your attention back to just noticing the thoughts that are present.

9. See if you can bring your attention to any action urges you are experiencing. Focus on just noticing these urges as they rise and fall, bringing attention to the ways they change or stay the same.

10. Keep focusing on the different components of your emotion without escaping or avoiding them. Continue to just notice your sensations, thoughts, and action urges without trying to push them away or change them. Do this for about ten to fifteen minutes, or until the emotion subsides and you no longer feel angry.

Now that you have practiced mindfully attending to your anger, it's time to identify the different components of your anger. Identifying the components will help you be more aware of your anger at lower levels of intensity—when it's easier to manage.

Increasing Your Awareness of the Different Components of Anger

As we mentioned earlier, all emotions are made up of three different components: physical, cognitive, and behavioral. Becoming more aware of each component will make it easier for you to recognize anger earlier.

Physical component. As we mentioned in chapter 1, emotions are full-body responses. Therefore, the physical sensations and bodily changes that go along with an emotion can be some of the earliest signs that you're experiencing an emotion. What these sensations feel like depends on the emotion you're experiencing, as different emotions are associated with different physical sensations.

The types of sensations that tend to go along with anger involve arousal and activation. Anger is an energizing emotion, so most people experience an increase in energy and agitation when they are angry. Use exercise 4.3 to help you identify the physical sensations associated with anger for you.

Exercise 4.3   Identifying Physical Sensations Associated with Anger

What does anger feel like in your body? Mark all of the physical sensations that apply for you.

☐ Racing or pounding heart

☐ Shortness of breath or shallow breathing

☐ Muscle tension

☐ Tension in the jaw

☐ Clenched teeth

☐ Feeling hot

☐ Feeling flushed in the face

☐ Increased perspiration or sweating

☐ Dry mouth

☐ Tightness in the chest

☐ Clenched fists

☐ Tunnel vision

Do you experience other physical sensations not listed above? Please note them below.

_____

_____

_____

- ## Thomas's Story

One reason Thomas struggled with anger was that it seemed to come out of nowhere. He'd be fine, and the next moment he'd be in a rage. Half the time he didn't know he was angry until he was screaming at someone. When his therapist first asked him what anger felt like in his body, he didn't have an answer. He only knew how he acted when he felt angry. This changed once he learned mindfulness skills. The more he practiced paying attention to his emotions, the more he noticed small changes that occurred in his body when he was beginning to feel angry. Soon he was able to recognize these physical sensations as early signs that he was feeling angry. And noticing his anger earlier made it easier to regulate.

Cognitive component. Although many of the situations listed in exercise 4.1 would provoke anger in a lot of people, how we think about and interpret these situations can influence how angry we feel. The interpretations you have can make the difference between feeling very angry, mildly annoyed, or not angry at all. For example, many people feel anger when they don't get what they asked for. Even though anger is a common reaction to being told no, it's not the only reaction people can have. It all comes down to how one interprets the situation. If you believe that you deserve what you're asking for and have a right to get it, you're probably going to feel anger if someone says no to a request you make. On the other hand, if you don't believe that you deserve what you asked for, or you think it was a selfish or silly request, you might feel guilty or embarrassed if someone says no. The bottom line is that our interpretation of a situation is often just as important to the emotion we experience as the situation itself.

As we mentioned in chapter 1, the thoughts that often go along with anger tend to focus on people, things, or the world around us being unfair, unjust, wrong, or simply not as we believe they should be. In fact, the presence of the words "should" or "unfair" in your mind are excellent clues that you may be experiencing an anger-related thought. So the next time you find yourself thinking that something shouldn't have happened, or that things should be different, or that someone should be doing something else, or that things aren't fair, take a step back and consider whether or not you are feeling anger. Catching it early on—before it becomes incredibly intense—will make it easier to regulate.

Even though thoughts of *should* and *unfair* often go hand in hand with feelings of anger for many people, there are all kinds of thoughts that go along with anger. What's more, some of the thoughts that go along with anger for you might be different from the thoughts that accompany anger for others. In order to learn more about your own personal experience of anger, it's important to figure out the specific thoughts that tend to accompany feelings of anger for you. Exercise 4.4 will help you do this.

Exercise 4.4   Identifying the Thoughts That Go Along with Anger

What kind of thoughts and interpretations accompany feelings of anger for you? Do you find yourself thinking certain words or phrases? Mark all of the thoughts and interpretations below that are associated with anger for you.

- ☐ This shouldn't have happened.

- ☐ This isn't fair.

- ☐ This isn't right.

- ☐ That person shouldn't have done that.

- ☐ What a jerk!

- ☐ I hate _____.

- ☐ This is so unfair.

- ☐ That person should be _____ (for example, doing something different, doing something else).

- ☐ This person or situation is wrong.

- ☐ Everyone is against me.

Are there any other thoughts that often go through your mind when you're angry? Please list them below.

_____

_____

_____

_____

_____

Behavioral component. The behavioral component of an emotion may actually be the first one you notice as you work on increasing your awareness of anger. Even before you notice the thoughts going through your mind or your physical sensations, you might be aware of your urges to do something or to act in a certain way. In fact, there might even be times when you don't realize you're feeling angry until you've acted on your anger in some way, for example, by screaming at a friend or punching a wall. Although the skills in this book will help you become more aware of all components of your anger, the first component to make it into your awareness may very well be the urges you're experiencing or the actions you take.

So, when you experience anger, what do you want to do? Do you have an urge to respond in a certain way? Do you want to scream or throw or hit something? Use the first half of exercise 4.5 to help you identify the action urges that go along with feelings of anger for you. Next, think about the types of things you actually do when you feel anger. How do you tend to act when you're angry? The second half of the exercise will help you identify the things you regularly do when you're angry. Identifying both of these behavioral components will help you better manage your anger.

Exercise 4.5 Identifying the Action Urges and Actions That Go Along with Anger

What types of things do you want to say or do when you feel anger? Mark all of the action urges associated with anger for you.

☐ Pick a fight

☐ Raise your voice

☐ Scream

☐ Throw something

☐ Punch or hit something

☐ Stand up for yourself

☐ Assert your needs

☐ Destroy something

☐ Protect someone

☐ Hurt yourself

☐ Confront someone

☐ Voice your opinion

Please list any other action urges not listed above.

_____

_____

_____

Next, think about the types of things you actually do when you feel anger. How do you tend to act? Make sure you check off everything you tend to do when you feel angry, both positive and negative. Identifying the healthy ways you express anger is just as important as figuring out the ways that don't work as well. Doing so can highlight the strengths and skills you already have as well as those areas you may need to work on.

☐ Pick a fight

☐ Raise your voice

☐ Scream

☐ Throw something

☐ Punch or hit something

☐ Stand up for yourself

☐ Assert your needs

☐ Protect someone

☐ Hurt yourself

☐ Confront someone

☐ Voice your opinion

☐ Destroy something

☐ Take action

☐ Threaten others

☐ Criticize others

☐ Stand up for someone else

☐ Beat yourself up

☐ Complain

Please list any other actions not listed above.

_____

_____

_____

Now that you've completed this exercise, take a moment to reflect on what you've learned. You may notice that some of the action urges overlap with the actions you identified, but others do not. For example, you might notice urges to raise your voice and yell when you feel anger, and you might find that this is something you do a lot when you're angry. On the other hand, you might have other urges, such as urges to punch someone or destroy something, that you've never acted on.

RECOGNIZING ANGER IN THE MOMENT

Now that you have a better understanding of the different components of anger and what this emotion is like for you, it's time to improve your awareness of your anger in the moment. Although thinking back to times you've felt anger in the past can provide a lot of useful information about how you experience anger, you may not have been paying attention to all of the components of anger that we reviewed here, or you may have forgotten some of the experiences. One of the best ways to get to know your anger better is to monitor it as it is happening. This process will help you become more aware of the bodily sensations, thoughts, action urges, and actions that go along with anger for you.

Worksheet 4.1 will help you monitor your anger. We recommend downloading additional copies of the worksheet (available at http://www.newharbinger.com/30215) so you can complete it each time you feel anger. After writing down the day and time in the first column, try to identify the situation that led to your anger. Use the DBT skill of objectively labeling your experience (Linehan 1993b, 2015) to describe the situation without judgment. Next, see if you can identify the bodily sensations, thoughts, and action urges associated with your anger. Focus on noticing each of these experiences and writing down everything you observe. Finally, write down what you did in response to the anger (the actions), both positive and negative.

Keep these monitoring forms with you throughout the day, and fill them out as soon as you can after you have noticed your anger. Monitoring your anger in the moment will provide the best information because the sensations, thoughts, action urges, and actions that go along with anger will be fresh in your mind.

Worksheet 4.1   Monitoring Anger

Day/Time	Situation	Bodily Sensations	Thoughts	Action Urges	Actions

Moving Forward

Our goal in this chapter was to help you become more aware of your anger so you can recognize it when it is less intense. Understanding your anger and learning to identify all of its components is a critical first step in learning to manage anger effectively. As scary as it may be, we want you to continue to practice the skills in this chapter so you can become more familiar with your anger. The more you understand your anger, the more you can reap its benefits and avoid its downsides.

In addition to recognizing your anger when it is less intense, another way to avoid the pitfalls of intense anger is to take steps to reduce your vulnerability to intense anger. We discuss these skills in the next chapter.

CHAPTER 5

Reducing Your Vulnerability to Intense Anger

Now that you have a better understanding of your own patterns of anger, it's time to talk about ways to reduce your vulnerability to intense anger. Even though anger can be a helpful emotion, managing anger—especially when that anger is intense and overwhelming—can seem like an insurmountable goal. The same is true for all emotions: Intense emotions of any kind are more difficult to manage and can tax the resources of even the most regulated person because strategies for regulating less intense emotions often don't work as well for strong ones. That's why reducing your vulnerability to intense anger is one effective strategy for making anger more manageable. If your anger is less intense, and if you experience it less frequently, you will be in a better position to manage it effectively when it does come up. The good news is there are a couple of different ways to go about reducing your vulnerability to intense anger, including taking care of your body and limiting your contact with anger-provoking situations.

TAKING CARE OF YOUR BODY

The first set of strategies is based on the fact that our minds and bodies are interconnected. How you feel physically has a big influence on your emotions and your ability to manage them. Think about the last time you were exhausted, or missed a meal, or had a really bad cold. How did those things influence your mood? Were you more edgy and easily frustrated? Were you more reactive? Did your emotions feel more overwhelming and out of control? Did you find that you were quicker to react in anger? Being tired, hungry, ill, or just "off" physically can make our emotions more intense and reactive. When we are physically dysregulated, our emotions are more likely to be dysregulated too.

Some researchers think that the ability to regulate emotions is a limited resource (Muraven and Baumeister 2000); it can be strengthened and replenished, but it is not infinite or unlimited. You can think of emotion regulation as a kind of muscle. For example, when you lift a heavy object, you will only be able to hold on to it for a certain period of time. Eventually, your muscles will give out and you will need to put it down. And while you are holding this object, and even for some time after you have put it down, you probably won't have the strength to lift other heavy objects. The same thing happens with the ability to regulate emotions: the more resources you need to devote to regulating your physical state, the fewer resources you'll have available to regulate your emotions and the less effective you'll be in managing them—especially when the emotions are intense.

One way to counteract this cycle is to take care of your body. Taking care of your body is one way to lower your baseline level of emotional arousal, or *emotional baseline*, so that you have more resources available to cope with the emotions or stressors you encounter throughout the day. Rather than walking around all day feeling on edge (and close to being pushed over!), you can start your day in a calmer and more relaxed state so you have a longer way to go before you reach your emotional threshold and the point of no return.

The importance of physical health for one's emotional well-being and the ability to manage emotions is so large that there is an entire set of DBT skills devoted to taking care of your body (Linehan 1993b, 2015). These skills will help ensure that you have more resources available to regulate any anger you experience.

Take care of illnesses. One simple way to maintain physical health is to take care of yourself when you are ill or feeling under the weather (Linehan 1993b, 2015). Being ill drains our bodies' resources quickly, making it harder to deal with the stressors and nuisances we experience throughout the day. And let's face it, feeling sick just isn't pleasant, which can make us more irritable. For these reasons, addressing any illnesses you have and taking steps to prevent illness and maintain overall physical health can put you in a much better position to manage your emotions and can even make you less reactive to anger-provoking situations. So, if you think you are coming down with something or know that you are sick, go to the doctor and get the help you need. If you are prescribed medications, be sure to take them as prescribed. If you are struggling with physical illness, go easy on yourself and take extra care of your body. Get extra sleep and drink a lot of liquids. Take a day off from work or give yourself a break on daily chores. Basically, do everything you can to take care of that illness and restore your physical health. You'll be amazed by how much more capable you feel of managing your anger when you are physically healthy.

Maintain balanced eating. Another way to ensure that you have as many resources available as possible to regulate anger is to maintain healthy eating habits (Linehan 1993b, 2015). Our bodies need nutrients not only to survive but to function at their best, so maintaining a healthy diet ensures that you have the fuel you need to cope with anger-provoking situations throughout the day.

Healthy eating is actually made up of two parts. The first part has to do with the spacing of meals and snacks throughout the day. Eating one or two large meals a day may give you energy for a while, but eventually you may find yourself running on fumes and less able to manage your anger. The other downside to eating only once or twice a day is that you may be so hungry by the time you do eat that you are at risk for overeating. And just like overeating can have unpleasant physical consequences, such as feeling uncomfortable and nauseated, it can take a toll on your emotional well-being as well, putting you in a bad mood and increasing your vulnerability to anger. The solution? Try to eat regularly throughout the day. This allows you to maintain a consistent source of energy—energy you can use to cope with difficult and stressful situations. Eating three meals and two snacks each day often works well.

The second part of healthy eating involves eating foods that are healthy and nutritious. This doesn't mean you need to give up your favorite junk food or sweet treat entirely. Any food can be part of a healthy diet if you eat it in moderation, and it's fine to allow yourself to splurge now and then with a piece of cheesecake or an order of fries. When it comes to giving your body the fuel it needs to function at its best, however, you need to eat a balanced diet with plenty of fruits, vegetables, whole grains, and proteins. These are the food groups that will provide your body with the nutrients and nourishment it needs to tackle the stressors you encounter each day.

Get enough sleep. In the same way your body needs proper nutrients to run well, it also needs enough sleep (Linehan 1993b, 2015). Sleep allows your body to restore its resources and build up the mental and physical energy it needs for the day ahead. If you don't get the full amount of sleep you need each night, your body won't have the time to fully restore its resources, which means you'll have fewer resources available to cope with daily nuisances and stressors. And this will likely put you on edge and make it much more difficult for you to manage your anger. In fact, a lot of people find that they are much more irritable and quicker to react with anger when they are sleep deprived. And if you are already someone who struggles with anger, sleep deprivation is only going to make managing anger more difficult.

Getting enough sleep—especially if you are on edge or struggling with ruminative thoughts—is much easier said than done. Fortunately, there are steps you can take to improve your sleep hygiene (Bourne 1995; Epstein et al. 2009; Linehan 2015).

- Keep a regular sleep schedule. Go to bed and get up at the same time each day. Stick to this schedule even if you don't feel ready to go to bed or feel too tired to get up. This practice will help get your body into a good sleeping rhythm. You also want to avoid taking naps during the day as this can greatly affect your ability to fall asleep at night.

- Eat your last meal a few hours before bedtime. Don't go to bed hungry, but don't eat right before you go to bed. Give your body time to digest the meal before you go to bed.

- If you exercise, do so in the morning or during the day. It's best to avoid exercising within six hours of your bedtime. Exercising right before bed can get your body revved up, making it more difficult to fall asleep.

- Limit the amount of caffeine you consume during the day. If you struggle to fall asleep at night, or if you know you are sensitive to caffeine, you may want to avoid caffeine completely after lunchtime. This includes foods that have caffeine, such as chocolate. Even though it may be hours before you go to bed, caffeine remains in your body for a long time. In fact, it takes your body five to six hours to process half the caffeine from a cup of coffee.

- Limit the amount of nicotine and alcohol you use, particularly close to bedtime. Although some people think smoking calms them, the relaxation people experience from smoking is really just a reduction in their cravings for nicotine. Smoking doesn't actually reduce stress. In fact, nicotine is a stimulant. Therefore, the more you smoke during the day, the harder it may be for you to fall asleep at night. This is particularly true if you smoke right before bed. Avoid having a cigarette right before bedtime. Similarly, avoid consuming alcohol within six hours of your bedtime, as this can increase arousal and keep you awake.

- Willing yourself to sleep doesn't work. In fact, trying to force yourself to sleep is probably going to increase your stress, making it even more difficult to fall asleep. If you find that you are still awake after being in bed for twenty to thirty minutes, get up and find something quiet and relaxing to do, such as reading a book. Keep in mind that the goal is to return to bed as soon as you start to feel drowsy, so choose something that can be stopped at any time. Watching television is generally not recommended, because some programs can be emotionally intense or can draw you in, making it even harder to get back to sleep.

- Avoid electronic devices, such as computers, smartphones, laptops, or tablets, in the hour or so before bed. The artificial light from these devices can trigger areas of your brain that are involved in wakefulness, making it more difficult to fall asleep. In addition, if these devices are connected with your work, school, or interpersonal problems in your life, using them may remind you of these stressors, serving as a cue for anger or causing your mind to start ruminating right before bedtime.

- Make your bedroom a relaxing and comfortable place. Keep it at a cool temperature. Buy noise-blocking earphones or an eye mask to block out any outside sounds or light. You may also want to limit the activities you do in your bedroom. Make it about sleep and sex and nothing else. Don't watch television in your bedroom or use your computer while in bed. You want your bedroom to be associated with sleep. This can help trigger your body to start the process of sleeping as soon as you go to bed.

As you start to make these changes, remember that developing healthier sleep patterns is a process. Changing your sleep habits isn't going to occur overnight, so don't get discouraged if you don't see immediate improvements in your sleep. The important thing is to commit to making changes. The better your sleep, the more resources you will have to manage any emotions that arise during the day.

Get regular exercise. There are a couple of reasons why regular exercise is so important for reducing your vulnerability to intense anger (Linehan 1993b, 2015). First, regular exercise can make your body stronger, building up your physical resources over time. This means that you will have more resources available for coping effectively with the hassles and stressors of everyday life.

The second reason has to do with the physical component of anger and the changes that occur in your body when you experience anger. As you may remember from chapter 1, anger is an energizing emotion that increases arousal and prepares us to act. For this reason, anger is often accompanied by a lot of physical energy. Therefore, releasing this energy in healthy ways is one way to reduce your vulnerability to intense anger. And one of the best ways to release energy is to exercise.

When we say that getting regular exercise is important, we don't mean that you have to work out at the gym several times a week. To reap the physical and emotional benefits of exercise, all you need is thirty minutes of some sort of moderate physical activity five days a week. Although going to the gym to run or use exercise equipment is one way to get exercise, there are many other ways of getting exercise. All that matters is that you get your heart rate up. In fact, the more flexible and creative you are about how to get your heart rate up, the better, because flexibility will give you more opportunities to get exercise even when you're busy and don't have time to get to the gym or an exercise class. So, focus on getting activity anywhere you can. If you have to go to the store, park as far away as possible so you can get in a bit of a walk. If you live or work in a multistory building, take the stairs rather than the elevator. When cleaning your house, focus on making the process as physical as possible, moving the vacuum vigorously and really throwing yourself into scrubbing the floors or polishing the furniture.

Limit alcohol and avoid drugs. Alcohol and drugs are mind- and mood-altering substances that can have a major toll on the body. Not only can they use up a lot of your body's physical resources, they can tax your emotional resources as well. Being under the influence of drugs or alcohol can also make you more likely to respond with anger. These substances lower inhibitions and make it more difficult to regulate emotions. In addition, the aftermath of alcohol or drug use—when you are no longer under the influence—can be very uncomfortable, which could put you on edge and make you irritable. For these reasons, limiting your intake of alcohol and avoiding drugs are helpful ways to reduce your vulnerability to intense anger (Linehan 1993b, 2015).

Increase self-efficacy by doing things that make you feel competent and in control. Have you ever noticed that when you feel good about yourself, you are less reactive to everyday hassles or less bothered by frustrating situations than you are when you feel negatively about yourself and your abilities? These are common experiences. How we feel about ourselves has a direct impact on our ability to handle stress and manage our emotional reactions to difficult situations. Fortunately, doing things each day that make you feel competent and in control will make you feel better about yourself (Linehan 1993b, 2015). Doing something that makes you feel in control is especially helpful for reducing vulnerability to intense anger. Some researchers believe that one of the functions of anger is to provide a sense of control, particularly when life feels out of control. Therefore, the more competent and in control you can feel throughout your day, the less you will need anger to give you that sense of control. So, cross something off your to-do list (or make a to-do list!), do something that you have been avoiding, do something you are good at, or do something that moves you toward a long-term goal. It doesn't matter what you do, as long as it makes you feel competent and in control.

Use exercise 5.1 to figure out what you are currently doing to take care of your body and the things you could change to help your body function at its best.

Exercise 5.1 Reducing Your Vulnerability to Intense Anger by Taking Care of Your Body

How well are you taking care of your body? If you answer yes to some of these activities, congratulations! You are taking care of your body and reducing your vulnerability to intense anger. If you answer no to some of these activities, think about how you can begin to take better care of yourself in these areas. Begin by identifying three specific actions you can take to improve your physical health. Making these changes will help ensure that you have the resources you need to cope with anger-provoking situations.

Activity	Please Circle One	Actions You Can Take to Improve Your Health
Do you go to the doctor for regular checkups?	Yes No	1. 2. 3.
Do you go to the doctor when you feel sick?	Yes No	1. 2. 3.
Do you take your medications as prescribed?	Yes No	1. 2. 3.
Do you eat several times throughout the day?	Yes No	1. 2. 3.

Do you eat fruits, vegetables, whole grains, and protein?	Yes No	1. 2. 3.
Do you limit junk food and sweets?	Yes No	1. 2. 3.
Do you get at least seven to nine hours of sleep per night?	Yes No	1. 2. 3.
Do you have a regular sleeping schedule?	Yes No	1. 2. 3.
Do you do some sort of physical activity every day?	Yes No	1. 2. 3.
Do you exercise for at least thirty minutes five days a week?	Yes No	1. 2. 3.

Do you limit your alcohol intake?	Yes No	1. 2. 3.
Do you refrain from using mood-altering drugs?	Yes No	1. 2. 3.
Do you do at least one thing a day that makes you feel capable and in control of your life?	Yes No	1. 2. 3.

TAKING STEPS TO AVOID OR CHANGE ANGER-PROVOKING SITUATIONS

Another way to reduce your vulnerability to intense anger is to limit your contact with anger-provoking situations. Makes sense, right? If you didn't encounter as many situations that bring up anger, or if these situations were less frustrating, you probably wouldn't experience intense anger as often. Of course, we don't mean to suggest that it's possible to avoid entirely situations that elicit anger. We live in a world where we encounter people, situations, and even objects that block us from reaching our goals or threaten our well-being. This is unavoidable. However, it is possible to take steps to avoid some of these situations, encounter them less often, or make them less distressing when you do encounter them.

Limiting Your Contact with Anger-Provoking Situations

The first step in limiting your contact with anger-provoking situations is to identify the situations and experiences that tend to bring up anger for you. Focus on situations or experiences you encounter frequently. Are there certain situations you encounter that almost always lead to intense anger or have the potential to do so? Although assuming the worst about a situation can be a self-fulfilling prophecy, increasing the likelihood that you'll perceive that situation in a negative way, knowing the types of situations and experiences that often bring up anger for you can help you plan ahead. You may find it helpful to refer back to exercise 4.1 to help you identify the situations that are most relevant to you.

Next, come up with a plan for avoiding these situations or limiting your contact with them. For example, if driving in heavy traffic tends to make you angry, what can you do to avoid heavy traffic? Can you change your work schedule so you don't have to drive during rush hour? Can you take a less congested route to work? Or can you take public transportation instead?

Exercise 5.2   Limiting Contact with
Anger-Provoking Situations

Write down all of the situations or experiences that tend to elicit intense anger in you.	Write down up to five things you can do to avoid or limit your contact with these situations.
1.	1. 2. 3. 4. 5.
2.	1. 2. 3. 4. 5.
3.	1. 2. 3. 4. 5.

4.	1.
	2.
	3.
	4.
	5.
5.	1.
	2.
	3.
	4.
	5.
6.	1.
	2.
	3.
	4.
	5.
7.	1.
	2.
	3.
	4.
	5.

8.	1. 2. 3. 4. 5.
9.	1. 2. 3. 4. 5.
10.	1. 2. 3. 4. 5.

Changing Anger-Provoking Situations

As we mentioned before, it is not possible to avoid all anger-provoking situations. Take the example of driving in traffic. Although some people may be able to avoid this situation by taking public transportation, others may not have access to public transportation. Likewise, although some people have flexibility in their work schedules and may be able to avoid the morning and evening rush hour commutes, many people cannot. In fact, it is because so many workplaces have similar hours that we have rush hours to begin with! The good news is that even if you can't avoid an anger-provoking situation, you may be able to modify it so that it is less upsetting.

To begin, use the information from exercise 5.2 to identify all of the anger-provoking situations in your life that you probably can't avoid and write them in the first column of exercise 5.3 below. You'll probably notice that the first columns of both exercises look very similar. Even if you were able to come up with steps to limit your contact with the anger-provoking situations you identified in exercise 5.2, most are probably not entirely avoidable.

Next, come up with a plan to make each situation in the first column more tolerable. Focus on small steps you can take to make the situation less frustrating. For example, to make driving in heavy traffic more enjoyable, you could play your favorite music, sip on your favorite drink (nonalcoholic, of course!), or use the time in the car to practice deep breathing. Although you probably won't be able to make driving in traffic pleasurable, the goal is simply to make the experience less distressing so you are less vulnerable to intense anger.

As another example, let's say that interacting with a particular supervisor at work is a cue for your anger. It's probably not possible to avoid this person entirely (at least not without risking your job), but there may be things you can do to make your interactions with this person less distressing or disruptive. For example, you could avoid scheduling something that is stressful before and after meetings with this person. You could also set aside time before and after these meetings (even if it's just a few minutes) to do something relaxing or enjoyable, such as listening to your favorite song, looking at pictures on your phone or the Internet, or practicing deep breathing. In these moments, you could also focus your attention on the aspects of your job that you enjoy and that are meaningful to you. Finally, there are simple steps you could take to make the time you do spend with this person less distressing, such as wearing your most comforting shirt or sweater, sipping on your favorite coffee, or wearing your favorite perfume or cologne—basically, anything you can do to make the situation less unpleasant.

Exercise 5.3   Changing Anger-Provoking Situations

Write down all of the unavoidable situations that tend to bring up anger for you.	Write down up to five steps that may make these situations less frustrating and more tolerable.
1.	1. 2. 3. 4. 5.
2.	1. 2. 3. 4. 5.
3.	1. 2. 3. 4. 5.

4.	1.
	2.
	3.
	4.
	5.
5.	1.
	2.
	3.
	4.
	5.
6.	1.
	2.
	3.
	4.
	5.
7.	1.
	2.
	3.
	4.
	5.

8.	1.
	2.
	3.
	4.
	5.
9.	1.
	2.
	3.
	4.
	5.
10.	1.
	2.
	3.
	4.
	5.

Nice work! Taking steps ahead of time to modify anger-provoking situations so they are less frustrating and less distressing is definitely going to reduce your vulnerability to intense anger. And managing mild anger or frustration is a lot easier than managing intense anger. Just identifying the steps you can take to reduce your contact with situations that anger you is an important step on the road to recovery.

Moving Forward

In this chapter, we focused on skills you can use to reduce your vulnerability to intense anger. The less intense and less frequent your anger is, the easier it is to manage. Therefore, one of the first steps in learning how to manage your anger is to reduce your propensity to intense anger. You can do this by taking care of your body so you have more resources available to regulate your anger, limiting your contact with anger-provoking situations, and taking steps to make anger-provoking situations less frustrating and more palatable.

Although it's easier to manage less intense anger, there are many DBT skills that are incredibly useful for both managing intense anger and expressing it effectively. The next few chapters focus on these skills.

CHAPTER 6

Using Mindfulness Skills to Effectively Manage Anger

Managing overwhelming problems with anger is a lot like fumbling around in a dark room trying to find your way out. The most useful tool to have in that circumstance is probably a flashlight. When it comes to working on anger, mindfulness is a lot like that flashlight; it's an essential tool that will help light your way out of the dark room of anger. Mindfulness is an invaluable tool for managing anger:

- Mindfulness helps you predict and prevent problematic angry behavior. Paying attention to the signs and symptoms of anger, as well as its cues, allows you to catch yourself before you walk too far down the path to intense anger.

- Mindfulness helps you regulate and tolerate your anger. Paying close attention to the wave of anger as it rises, crests, and falls will help you realize that anger does not last forever, that nothing terrible has to happen because of your anger, and that you can tolerate anger and get through whatever situation you're in.

- Mindfulness helps you avoid doing things that make that wave of anger bigger, such as ruminating (discussed in chapters 1 and 9).

- Mindfulness gives you a sense of freedom from and power over your anger. If you practice paying attention to but not acting on your anger, you will develop a sense of freedom and control. Instead of being a helpless swimmer swallowed by the wave of anger, using mindfulness you can expertly ride the wave like a pro surfer.

- Mindfulness helps you let go of your attachment to the way things are or to the wish that things were different. Often people are angry because they are attached to the desire for situations, people, thoughts, emotions, and even themselves to be different. Rather than hopelessly clinging to a different reality, mindfulness helps you accept things as they are.

- ## Dave's Story

Dave came to therapy after he was fired from a job. He always knew that he had a bit of a fiery temper, but everything came to a head when he found out that two colleagues received small promotions and pay raises, whereas he did not. Dave had been at the job for the same amount of time and had not yet received any special recognition or a raise. He set up a meeting to talk with his boss about why he was passed over for promotions. His boss told him that he was disappointed with some aspects of Dave's work. Already feeling hurt and angry, Dave snapped and blew up, yelling and swearing at his boss. His boss gave him two weeks' notice, and Dave is currently looking for work. Dave's marriage is also under a lot of strain, because of both the financial situation and Dave's stress level and anger problems.

As you work your way through this chapter, we will discuss Dave's story to illustrate the ways you can use mindfulness skills to effectively manage anger.

MINDFULLY ATTENDING TO YOUR EXPERIENCES

Mindfulness involves paying attention to, contemplating, and noticing something while letting go of judgments and assumptions. To mindfully attend to something, you must take a step back in your mind and look at it objectively without evaluating it as good or bad or right or wrong. Don't try to change it. Instead, be open to the experience, regardless of whether you like or dislike it. This process is a lot like walking outside in the morning and paying attention to the weather—the warmth or coolness of the air, the clouds in the sky, even the feeling of rain—and not being attached to it being different. When it comes to anger or anger-provoking situations, attending to them is much easier said than done. We'll start with exercises to get you familiar with mindfully attending to your everyday experiences, and then you'll start applying these skills to anger.

Before you begin the exercises, we have one very important tip for you to keep in mind. When you're mindfully attending to one thing, your mind will almost always wander to something else. This is simply what minds do: they think, plan, worry, ruminate, daydream, fantasize, and so on. We try to focus on one thing, such as our morning coffee or a conversation, but our thoughts, memories, and feelings drag us away into our own heads. This is perfectly normal. In fact, the practice of mindfully attending to something is not about gluing your attention to something. Instead, the idea is to gently guide your attention back to whatever you're focusing on whenever your mind wanders. If you're paying attention to the birds and trees in the morning but notice yourself getting caught up in your to-do list for the day, gently guide your attention back to the birds and the trees. It's not easy to focus on one thing at a time, but as with lifting weights, the more you practice, the stronger your mindfulness muscles will become.

Try out the exercises below to get started with the skill of mindfully attending to your experiences. These exercises will not only help you get your feet wet with mindfulness, but if you practice them regularly, you might be able to bring mindful attention to more of your daily experiences. As a result, you will be more awake and attentive to each moment, both of which can allow you to reduce stress and get more out of life.

- Make a cup of coffee, tea, warm milk, or another hot beverage of your choice and, when the temperature is comfortable, place your hands around the cup and simply pay attention to the feeling of warmth and any smells rising from the beverage. Slowly bring the cup to your lips and notice the sensation of steam and warmth on your nose and face. Take a slow sip and notice what the liquid feels like in your mouth, what tastes arise, and how it feels to swallow.

- Sit outside in the morning in your backyard, on your porch, or in a park where you can see trees. Watch the birds as they fly from branch to branch and from tree to tree. Pay attention to the quality of their movements, their shape, their size, their color, and the sounds of their chirping.

- Go for a walk and pay attention to the sensations on the bottoms of your feet. Even if you experience pain, do your best to keep your attention anchored on the sensations, including pressure, temperature, and strain. Mindfully attend to these sensations without trying to adjust or change them (unless you have an injury).

When Dave began therapy, he told his therapist that he was not sure how this mindfulness stuff would help him with anger. He said he had tried relaxation, meditation, and many other coping skills before, and yet he still ended up blowing up at his boss and sometimes at his wife and children. His therapist encouraged him to give mindfulness a try anyway—to think of it as an experiment. Dave started by getting up before his wife and children in the morning so he would have quiet time to mindfully attend to his breakfast. Besides giving him a good chance to practice mindfulness, this new routine was great for stress reduction, as this was one of the few times of the day during which he could relax and have alone time. Although Dave's anger didn't magically disappear, he started to see value in practicing mindfulness.

MINDFULLY ATTENDING TO YOUR EMOTIONS

Once you've gotten your feet wet mindfully attending to everyday experiences, it's time to apply this skill to your emotions. As you may recall, we mentioned in chapters 1 and 4 that emotions have three different components. The physical is generally the easiest component to pay attention to. It includes muscle sensations, your heartbeat, your respiration, feelings of warmth or coolness, and feelings of heaviness or lightness, among many other physical responses. Mindfully attending to your emotions is one of the most powerful and effective emotion regulation skills DBT has to offer (Linehan 1993b, 2015).

One great place to start with this skill is exercise 4.2 in chapter 4. In that exercise we ask you to guide your attention to different areas of your body, zeroing in on where you notice emotions, including anger. By using this exercise when you have different types of emotional experiences, you can become attuned to the sensations that go along with a particular emotion. Once you've practiced doing all of the steps, you can graduate to the next level: rather than noticing only the sensations of an emotion, step back in your mind and mindfully attend to the thoughts and urges that accompany your emotions as they occur throughout the day.

To use this skill at the next level, you might want to start with happiness, excitement, or some other easier or more pleasant emotion. Whenever you feel one of these emotions to a moderate degree, bring your attention to your body and, with curiosity, simply notice whatever you experience. Avoid judging your emotion as good or bad or right or wrong. Other things to avoid with your emotion include holding on to it, pushing it away, avoiding or escaping it, changing it, or acting on it. Your main goal is to simply watch it come and go. Let the emotion rise and fall like a wave on the ocean.

After you have had practice observing pleasant emotions, the next challenge is to apply this skill to anger. It might be helpful to begin with exercise 4.2. Some people find that mindfully attending to anger is calming, so an added benefit of this exercise might be that you feel calmer and less stressed or angry once you are finished.

After seeing a therapist for a few weeks, Dave began to practice exercise 4.2 to mindfully attend to the sensations of his emotions. He discovered that he was carrying a lot of tension in his neck, shoulders, and jaw. This realization not only helped him become more aware of how he was experiencing his emotions, but it also helped him pinpoint areas that he should focus on when he practiced relaxation strategies.

Upgrading Your Radar to Notice Early Signs of Anger

Once you have practiced mindfully attending to your anger several times, the sensations that accompany it will become more familiar to you. This is important because, perhaps more so than other emotions, anger can creep up on you. Have you ever noticed yourself blowing up without warning or feeling much more angry than a situation warrants? Let's say you arrive home from work and feel incredibly angry about something that someone says. This reaction might have been avoided had you noticed the early signs of irritation and less intense anger during the day, because then you could have done something about your anger before going home. Often if you do a little detective work, you'll find signs that anger was building earlier in the day. If you think back on your day, you might realize that it was stressful and filled with a lot of seemingly minor annoyances. You might recall that several times during the day small amounts of frustration flared up.

Early signs of anger can be hard to pick up on. They include subtle changes in physiology (such as slight muscle tension), thoughts (such as negative thoughts and ruminating), or behavior (such as moving around more quickly). If you upgrade your emotional radar by practicing exercise 4.2, mindfully attending to your emotions, you will start to notice the early signs of anger, such as frustration. When you notice the early signs, you can do something about them in order to avoid a blowup. For example, when you notice frustration building at work, try some of the skills in this book, such as self-soothing, distraction, or opposite action. Or let's say you're at home having dinner and notice telltale signs that your anger is building. (In Dave's case, telltale signs were talking or moving around more quickly than usual.) You could gently excuse yourself from the table and do something to distract yourself or to reduce your anger before returning to the table.

Mindfully Riding the Wave of Anger

Another effective way to integrate mindfulness with anger management is to practice mindfully riding the wave of anger as you go about your daily life. Here's how:

- The next time you feel angry, frustrated, or irritated, step back in your mind and turn your attention to how your body feels. See if you can tell where the sensations of anger are most noticeable. Focus your attention on the sensations without judging them or trying to change or get rid of them.

- Notice whether you are experiencing any of the urges to take action that we discussed in chapters 1 and 4, such as yelling at someone, criticizing someone, snapping at someone, or getting physically aggressive.

- Experience your emotions without acting on them. Emotions are a lot like waves that you can ride out. They rise and fall relatively quickly as long as you don't do anything to retrigger them, such as staying in an anger-provoking situation or ruminating. Simply step back and allow that wave to rise and fall without acting on your urges. You might choose to use your imagination, envisioning yourself as a surfer riding the wave of anger to shore. (This strategy of riding out your anger is similar to the strategy of *urge surfing* described by Marlatt and Gordon 1985.)

When first practicing riding out your anger, it is a good idea to be cautious about what you do or say next. When you are in the middle of a situation that is making you angry, often the best thing to do is to stop doing or saying anything. Of course, if you're in the middle of a discussion with someone, it might be a little odd to stop talking in order to mindfully ride out the emotion! But it is perfectly okay to pause, take a short breath, and ride out the wave of anger until you're able to do or say something effective.

Once you ride out the wave of anger, the next step is to use a skill that will help you do one of three things: (1) avoid doing anything that makes the situation worse, (2) effectively communicate to the person you're dealing with, or (3) leave the situation until you are able to come back with a clear and wiser mind-set. We cover these skills in other chapters, but we mention them here so you can see how they will come into play once you have practiced mindfully attending to your anger.

Like most people, when Dave first started mindfully attending to his anger, he did not find it easy. For example, one day he was working on his taxes when his son began screaming and yelling at his sister in another room. Since his wife was dealing with the fight, Dave closed the door, put on a white-noise machine, and tried to focus on his taxes. Unfortunately, the screaming continued, and Dave began to feel very frustrated. He remembered that this was an ideal time to practice the skill of mindfulness, so he tried his best to step back in his mind and pay attention to the sensations of his frustration and anger. It took every ounce of his willpower to not run into the other room and yell at his children to be quiet. He did, however, manage to ride out the wave of anger without acting on it. Even though the screaming in the other room continued, after a few minutes the wave had mostly crashed.

OBJECTIVELY LABELING YOUR EXPERIENCES

As we discussed in chapter 2, the skill of objectively labeling your experiences involves simply describing your experiences in a neutral way, sticking to the facts, and avoiding judgments or assumptions. When it comes to anger, this mindfulness skill can be invaluable for a few key reasons:

- It will help you accurately name your emotions, and simply naming your emotional state might help reduce activity in the emotional areas of your brain.

- It will help you avoid thoughts, judgments, and assumptions that can add fuel to the fire of your anger.

- It will help you better understand your own patterns of anger, which will give you a sense of mastery over anger and help you better communicate your feelings to others.

One important rule for using the skill is that you can only label things that you can actually see, hear, taste, smell, or touch (Linehan 1993b, 2015). Yet there are many things that people try to label even though they can't actually sense them. For example, some people spend a lot of time making assumptions about the personalities and behaviors of others. Consider times when you have tried to describe the thoughts, feelings, or intentions of someone else. Did you actually see, hear, taste, smell, or touch these things? Probably not. It's more likely that you were making assumptions. Not even psychologists can jump into their clients' heads to see what they are feeling or thinking or to know why they are behaving a certain way. Still, many of us spend a fair amount of time making assumptions about what other people think or feel.

We also spend a fair amount of time judging ourselves, our experiences, or others as good or bad or right or wrong. Judging also comes in the form of statements about the way things should or should not be: *My partner should pick up his socks instead of leaving them on the floor! My kids shouldn't scream so much. People shouldn't drive so slowly. My friend should be more thoughtful.*

Judging is a natural human tendency. We probably learned to judge because it is an efficient way of dealing with the world. Instead of going into a long explanation of how the fish on your plate looks green, furry, and slimy, you can simply say, "This fish looks bad." You're not saying that the fish is morally corrupt, or that it was mean to other fish when it was alive, but that the fish looks rotten, and if you eat it you might get sick. In this way, judging is a very useful shortcut that helps us quickly categorize things as either helpful or harmful.

The problem is that judging can go awry in a couple of important ways. First, when you judge yourself, your experiences, or other people as bad, you are adding fuel to the fire of your anger. If somebody does something that you don't like and you exclaim in your mind that the person is *bad* or *stupid*, your anger will only get worse. Perhaps you've noticed this happening in your own life. We talk more about thinking patterns in chapter 9.

Second, thinking or stating that something shouldn't be the way it is can make your anger worse. For example, if you are frustrated because someone painted your living room the wrong color and you get caught up in thoughts that it shouldn't be this way, you will probably become even more frustrated. Thinking that the paint shouldn't be the way it is doesn't change it; it only inflames your anger.

Oftentimes our assumptions and judgments are the *primary* fuel for our anger. Much of the time, we may not even notice that we're making assumptions and judgments. For example, my coauthor (A. L. Chapman) told me that he has been working for a number of years on walking more slowly. He found himself darting quickly from place to place, both at work and at home, almost like a squirrel in a tree or a yard. It seemed like his goal was to shave off precious seconds when moving from one place to the next. This approach to walking led to a fair amount of stress and tension, because inevitably there was somebody walking much more slowly in front of him. Sometimes these people were very hard to get around. People standing in the middle of doorways nearly drove him mad.

He realized that it was normal to feel frustrated when he was in a hurry and someone was in his way. What he didn't notice, however, was how he was thinking about these people—until he sat down and really thought about it. He found that he was making a lot of assumptions and judgments—such as assuming that these people were purposely getting in his way, or judging them as foolish for standing in doorways. When he realized this, he started to objectively label his experiences to make it easier to tolerate people in his way. He had to drop his assumptions and judgments and simply describe what was happening. For example, *I'm walking quickly and there is someone in front of me* had a dramatically different effect on his frustration level than *This person is crazy. Why doesn't she get out of my way?* or *Doesn't she know you're not supposed to stand in doorways?!*

To objectively label your experiences, you have to be willing to let go of judgments and assumptions and stick to the facts at hand. In fact, a good mind-set to get into when labeling (or even mindfully attending to) your experience is one that is both open to your current experience and very concrete. This may sound simple, but it's not easy.

We find it helpful to think about animals in the wild that are incredibly alert and attentive. For example, a frog will sit perfectly still for the longest time, carefully observing the environment and waiting for a fly or other insect to come along. Frogs are also incredibly alert to their surroundings and will react quickly to get out of harm's way. Moreover, as far as we can tell, frogs are concrete thinkers. They don't make assumptions about the motives or intentions of other creatures; they don't judge situations or other creatures as good or bad or right or wrong. Frogs simply observe and react accordingly. So if anybody ever calls you a frog or says that you are toad-like, take it as a compliment! Maybe you've really honed your mindfulness skills.

To get started with the skill of objectively labeling your experiences, try this exercise:

1. Think about a recent situation that mildly or moderately annoyed you. Don't start with a situation that left you enraged or extremely angry.

2. On a piece of paper, describe exactly what happened in that situation. What was annoying about it? Who was there, and what were they doing? Take some time to simply describe exactly what happened.

3. Look over your description and circle anything that is not a concrete fact. This means you'll be circling words or phrases such as "good," "bad," "right," "wrong," "should," "shouldn't," "wanted to," "likes to," among others. See if you can make it like a game to find and circle your judgments and assumptions.

4. Now imagine there's a very sophisticated video recording system that not only records exactly what happens but also describes it like a story. This video recording system is essentially a computer, and it is completely objective. It doesn't judge anyone or anything, and it doesn't make assumptions about other people's intentions or motives. How would the video recording system describe your situation? Rewrite your description exactly that way, sticking completely to objective facts.

5. Describe how you felt in the situation. Start with the physical component of your emotion, describing how it felt physically. Then describe what thoughts (cognitive component) were going through your mind at the time. Finally, describe any action urges (behavioral component) you had as well as what you actually did. See if you can get in touch with the space—even if it is really small—between your action urge and your action. There is always such a space. See if you can connect with the fact that you are free to not act on these urges. In fact, you are free to do whatever you think will be most effective in any situation.

Dave eventually started a new job where he worked in close quarters with a few people in cubicles. One colleague tended to talk very loudly on the phone with her husband when the supervisor was not around. Dave found this extremely distracting and irritating. Whenever she started talking, Dave noticed anger bubbling up inside. It dawned on him that these moments offered the perfect opportunity to practice the mindfulness skills he was learning. He started by mindfully attending to his experience, and then he objectively labeled the experience and the feelings it brought forth. To do this, he had to let go of the thoughts that were adding fuel to his anger, such as that this woman was being inconsiderate and lazy and was intentionally trying to make his life hard. When he let go of these judgments, he still felt frustrated, but his feelings were much less intense. In fact, because he was able to get his frustration to a manageable level, he was able to think clearly and figure out what to do about the situation. He chose a time when he felt fairly calm, and over coffee he brought up his concerns with the woman in a kind way, letting her know how her conversations on the phone were distracting him. Unexpectedly, she apologized and became tearful, telling him about some of the difficulties she and her husband were having. Through this conversation they got to know each other better. She changed her behavior, and Dave avoided the kinds of blowups he had experienced in many other similar situations in the past.

Moving Forward

It can surprise people to learn that such a simple set of skills can make such a huge difference in life, and yet that is definitely the case when it comes to mindfulness. In fact, DBT practitioners consider mindfulness the fundamental skill upon which all other skills are based. Of course, just because something is simple doesn't mean it is easy, and mindfulness takes a lot of practice. With practice, however, you will begin to see benefits. Mindfully attending to your experiences will help you ride the wave of your anger, learning to master and tolerate it rather than act on it. The skill of objectively labeling will help you let go of judgments and assumptions that make that wave of anger bigger. This skill will also help you get in touch with the concrete facts of anger-provoking situations, which is an essential step if you want to work on changing those situations and your reactions to them. It is important to remember that this chapter simply provides you with a starting point—the first few steps in your practice of mindfulness. Mindfulness can be a lifelong practice, something you work on each day. In our experience, the regular practice of mindfulness doesn't just help us regulate or respond to intense emotions more effectively, it also brings happiness, joy, and a sense of freedom to our everyday lives.

We are confident that with regular practice you'll start noticing the benefits of mindfulness as well. One of the first benefits you might notice is that you have space between the emotional reaction of anger and your response to it. Within that space you can decide to do something that makes the situation better rather than worse. That is the focus of the next chapter, in which we guide you through important skills you can use to avoid making things worse when you're angry.

CHAPTER 7

How to Avoid Making Things Worse When You're Angry

As you've probably figured out by now, feeling anger isn't a problem in and of itself. Anger is a normal human emotion that all people experience, and getting in touch with feelings of anger can give you the motivation you need to tackle problems head-on and to stand up for yourself and others.

What can be problematic, though, are the ways that people express their anger or the things they do when they're angry. When people experience anger, they often have urges to act in ways that won't be effective and could actually make a situation worse. Look back at exercise 4.5 in chapter 4. Do you notice that many of the action urges associated with anger involve behaviors that are destructive? That's one reason why it can be so difficult to avoid making things worse when you're feeling angry. Anger comes with all kinds of action urges to engage in behaviors that can get people in trouble. That's why one of the best things you can do when you're experiencing intense anger is to avoid acting on your urges. Not acting on your anger when you're most angry can protect you from some of the downsides of anger and keep you out of trouble.

The skills in this chapter are designed to help you avoid acting on intense anger so you don't make thing worse.

LEAVE THE SITUATION

The good news is that one of the best ways to avoid making things worse when you're angry is also the simplest: leave the situation. It's hard to make things worse when you're not there. So, if you are not sure what skills to use or how best to manage your anger in a particular situation, remove yourself from the situation (Linehan 1993b, 2015). Although simple, this can be an incredibly powerful tool, providing the time and space you need to figure out how best to respond and giving your anger a chance to become less intense.

As we mentioned in chapter 1, emotions always pass. That's one thing about emotions you can count on. Although it can feel like your anger will last forever, emotions are not long lasting. No matter how intense they feel at certain times, emotions always pass. For this reason, simply buying yourself some time will give your anger a chance to subside. Leaving the situation also provides distance between you and whatever cued your anger so that your anger doesn't get retriggered.

So how exactly do you go about leaving a situation? Well, that depends on the situation and who else, if anyone, is involved. This skill is easiest to use when you're by yourself. In those instances, all you need to do is walk away. Walking away becomes more difficult if another person is involved. If that's the case, then how you leave depends a lot on your relationship with the person and how much she or he knows about your struggles with anger. If the situation involves a close friend or family member who is aware of your difficulties with anger, you can inform that person in advance that you're working on your anger. You can explain that if you notice intense anger and aren't sure what to do, you're going to leave the situation to avoid making things worse. Then, the next time you're angry and decide to use this skill, you can either remind the person that this is what you're doing or simply excuse yourself and walk away.

Sometimes the situation that's making you angry will involve someone you don't know as well or who doesn't know you're working on your anger. To prepare for these situations, it can be helpful to plan in advance simple things you can say to excuse yourself. Saying that you need to use the restroom or take a phone call or even retrieve something in the other room can be effective ways to leave gracefully and quickly. And if you plan them in advance, you won't need to come up with them on the spot when you're feeling really angry. That said, as helpful as it can be to plan in advance ways to excuse yourself, there are going to be times when the only thing you can do is quickly remove yourself from the situation. At times like these, it's usually better to leave a situation abruptly, even if your exit is not graceful, than to act on urges to do something destructive.

Of course, leaving the situation is only the first step. What you do once you've left the situation is just as important. Below are some tips for making this skill work for you.

Tip 1: Focus on Something Other Than What Angered You

Now that you've left the situation, it's time to focus your attention on something else. Using the DBT skills of distraction (Linehan 1993b) will give your anger time to subside. Distracting yourself will also keep you from retriggering your anger by ruminating about what made you angry. Think about it: if you use your time away from the situation to obsess about what made you angry or get caught up in angry thoughts, you are going to maintain your anger and prevent it from passing. The goal is to focus your attention elsewhere so your anger can begin to pass. There are a number of DBT distraction skills that can help with this (Linehan 1993b, 2015).

Do something. One of the best ways to distract yourself from an anger-provoking situation is to throw yourself into an activity that captures your attention (Linehan 1993b, 2015). Focusing on such an activity will help keep your mind off of whatever is angering you. One nice thing about this skill is that the possibilities are endless. You can choose almost any activity as long as it is interesting, stimulating, or hard to ignore.

- **Do something physically demanding.** Throwing yourself into an activity that pushes your body and requires a lot of physical energy keeps your attention focused on your body and the activity at hand. An added benefit of physically demanding activities, such as aerobics, rock climbing, hiking, or swimming, is that they help burn off some of the energy that goes along with feelings of anger.

- **Do an outdoor activity.** Many people find that being outdoors is a good distraction. When you're outdoors there are all kinds of things that can capture your attention, from the temperature and feel of the air to the sounds you hear to the sights around you to the things you smell. And the more senses an activity captures, the more it will grab your attention. So if you need a distraction, take a walk and notice what you see, feel, hear, and smell. Rake your yard. Shovel snow. Watch kids play. Try to identify the birds you see and hear. Focus on observing the sights and sounds around you.

- **Do some work.** Throwing yourself into work that you need to get done can be a great distraction. Not only can it take your mind off whatever angered you, it has the added benefit of helping you accomplish something, which in and of itself can reduce your stress and make it easier to manage intense emotions. So find a chore or task that you need to get done and focus all of your attention on it. Do the laundry that has piled up. Clean the bathroom. Balance your checkbook. Mow the lawn. Work on your homework from school or therapy. It doesn't matter what you do as long as you focus all of your attention on completing it.

- **Do something you enjoy.** Doing something you enjoy is another great distraction because it is likely to capture your attention. What's more, experiencing emotions that are the opposite of anger, such as joy, happiness, or contentment, can help your anger subside. So do something you like! Get a meal at your favorite restaurant. Hang out with a good friend. Watch your favorite television show or movie. Engage in your favorite hobby. Go shopping or to a museum. As long as you choose something you really enjoy, you can't go wrong.

Get your mind busy. One of the best ways to distract yourself from anger is to give your mind something else to focus on (Linehan 1993b, 2015). Although getting active and throwing yourself into an activity can be a really helpful skill, it can be difficult to keep your mind from returning to whatever upset you. Just because your body is active doesn't mean your mind will follow suit. If you keep your mind busy, however, it won't have a chance to think about anything else. There are many ways to keep your mind busy.

- **Make your mind work.** If your mind is working hard, there won't be time for it to focus on the situation that angered you. The key is to get your mind engaged in an activity that requires focus. Do math equations in your head. Starting at zero, keep adding seven until you exceed one hundred; then begin subtracting seven until you reach zero again. Repeat this process. Do a crossword puzzle or word game. Play a challenging game on your phone. Play a stimulating computer game that really makes you think. Count the holes in the ceiling tiles. Count the clicks of the second hand on a clock. Try to come up with the name of an animal or a city that starts with each letter of the alphabet.

- **Think about something else.** If your mind is focused on something else, it can't focus on the situation that made you angry. Think about a positive experience you've had, or something that made you laugh. Think about food you like or people you care about. Think about a pet you had and silly things it did. Think about what you need to do in the coming week.

- **Use your imagination.** Give your mind something really captivating and positive to focus on. Imagine your favorite vacation spot or the place you'd most like to visit. See if you can really picture yourself there. Imagine something you've always wanted to do and picture yourself doing it. Try to bring to mind all of the sights, sounds, smells, and touch sensations you would experience in this situation. Imagine someone you are attracted to or a celebrity you'd like to spend time with.

Create strong sensations. Another way to keep yourself from focusing on whatever made you angry is to create a sensation that is so powerful or strong that you can't help but focus on it (Linehan 1993b). Really intense sensations can jolt you out of your head and capture your attention. At some point, it's just not possible to ignore an intense sensation. Your attention is pulled to the sensation and, as a result, away from anything else. One nice thing about this skill is that you can focus on any of your five senses, although we find that taste, smell, and touch tend to work best. There are many ways to create strong sensations.

- **Taste.** Suck on candy with a very strong flavor, such as spicy cinnamon or sour lemon. Place a very small amount of wasabi paste on your tongue and notice the feelings. Bite into a raw jalapeño pepper or suck on a lemon.

- **Smell.** Seek out smells that are really strong or potent. Some people find that unpleasant smells are more distracting than pleasant ones. Slice an onion and breathe in the fumes. Buy scratch-and-sniff stickers and use the unpleasant-smelling ones. Open a bottle of vinegar and breathe deeply. Light a bunch of scented candles with different strong fragrances all at once. Spray strongly scented perfume or cologne in the air or on yourself.

- **Touch.** Focus on sensations that are jarring and capture your attention. Hold a piece of ice in your hand until it melts, or hold it against your neck or forehead. Hold on to a plastic bag filled with ice cubes until you can't take it anymore. Take a cold shower. Sit in a cold bath. While in the shower, turn the temperature back and forth from hot to cold. Run outside on a really cold day with light clothing on.

- **Sound.** Listen to loud music that is upbeat or happy. Listen to your favorite song and sing along. Listen to music that gives you a jolt, such as loud heavy metal if you're not used to it. Find sounds on your computer or the Internet and play them at a very loud volume. Blow a whistle.

- **Sight.** Focus on an image that really captures your attention. Look at pictures with vibrant colors and strong lines. Look at artwork that you find compelling. Watch an exciting video or something you really enjoy. Focus your attention on every aspect of the image, artwork, or video.

Now that you've learned all kinds of skills to focus your attention on something other than what made you angry, it's time to put them into action! As we mentioned earlier, the key to distraction is to do something that captures your attention and takes your mind off your anger and the anger-provoking situation. Therefore, it's important to try out various activities to see just how captivating they are. Although what works best to distract you will probably depend on the particular situation, some distraction skills will probably work better for you than others. Use exercise 7.1 to determine the best ones for you.

Exercise 7.1 Skills for Distracting Yourself When You Are Angry

Use this exercise to help you figure out which of the distraction skills we reviewed in this chapter work best for you.

First, rate the intensity of your anger on a scale of 0 (no anger at all) to 10 (the most intense anger ever) in the "Anger Before" column. Now try out some of the distraction skills listed in the left column. After you use each skill, immediately rate your anger again on a scale from 0 to 10 in the "Anger After" column. After you have done this a few times, you might notice that some strategies do a better job of distracting you than others.

Distraction Skill		Anger Before (0 to 10)	Anger After (0 to 10)
Do something.			
	Do something physically demanding.		
	Do an outdoor activity.		
	Do some work.		
	Do something you enjoy.		
Get your mind busy.			
	Make your mind work.		
	Think about something else.		
	Use your imagination.		

Create strong sensations.			
	Taste		
	Smell		
	Touch		
	Hearing		
	Sight		

Comments: Include any comments on what you tried, what did or did not work for you, and what you might do the next time you want to distract yourself from something that angered you.

Tip 2: Focus on the Downsides of Acting on Urges to Engage in Destructive Behaviors

One reason it can be so difficult for people to control their behavior when they're angry is that expressing intense anger can feel really good in the moment. Even though reacting out of anger can make things a lot worse in the long term, it often provides a sense of release and much-needed relief in the short term.

One way you can motivate yourself to avoid acting on urges to do something destructive is to focus on the fact that doing so will only make things worse. Considering that you're probably feeling fairly distressed to begin with when you're experiencing intense anger, we're guessing you wouldn't want to add to your problems or feel even more upset. Focusing on all of the negative consequences you'll experience if you react out of anger can help you control your behavior and choose more effective ways to act (Linehan 1993b, 2015). This skill is similar to the pros and cons skill (Linehan 1993b) we discussed in chapter 3, except that here we're asking you to focus all of your attention on just the cons of acting on urges to do something destructive. Use exercise 7.2 to identify the negative consequences of acting on these urges.

Exercise 7.2   The Negative Consequences of Acting on Urges to Engage in Destructive Behaviors

The following list contains a number of negative consequences people may experience if they act on urges to do something destructive. Mark all that apply to you. Then, write down other negative consequences you experienced in the past when you reacted out of anger.

RELATIONSHIP CONSEQUENCES

- ☐ Increased conflict

- ☐ Damaged trust

- ☐ Hurting other people's feelings

- ☐ Damaged relationships

- ☐ Breakups

- ☐ Loss of friendships

- ☐ Increased isolation

List other negative consequences for relationships below.

1. _____

2. _____

3. _____

4. _____

5. _____

6. _____

EMOTIONAL CONSEQUENCES

- ☐ Guilt

- ☐ Shame

- ☐ Anger toward self

- ☐ Loneliness

- ☐ Fear

List other negative emotional consequences below.

1. _____

2. _____

3. _____

4. _____

5. _____

6. _____

CONSEQUENCES IN OTHER AREAS (WORK, SCHOOL, LEGAL)

- ☐ Loss of a job

- ☐ Arrest or incarceration

- ☐ Loss of a promotion or raise

- ☐ Warnings or disciplinary actions at work

- ☐ Suspension from school

- ☐ School detention

List other negative consequences below.

1. _____

2. _____

3. _____

4. _____

5. _____

6. _____

Now that you've identified the downsides of reacting out of intense anger, keep this list with you and review it whenever you're having urges to do something destructive. As we discussed in chapter 3, connecting with all of the downsides of acting on these urges will help motivate you to use the other skills in this book to express your anger in more effective ways.

Tip 3: Focus on the Upsides of Not Acting on Urges to Engage in Destructive Behaviors

The flip side of focusing on the downsides of acting on urges to do something destructive is to connect with the positive consequences of controlling your behaviors and not acting on urges to engage in destructive behaviors, no matter how angry you feel (Linehan 1993b, 2015). Although you probably wouldn't be reading this book if you weren't already aware of some of the benefits of expressing anger differently, motivation to change patterns and use new skills can wax and wane over time. Focusing on the positive consequences of not acting on urges to do something destructive is a useful skill for increasing your motivation to express anger more effectively.

Now, we don't recommend trying to come up with these positive consequences when you're really angry. At those times, you're going to be much more drawn to the short-term benefits of acting on your urges, and it's going to be a lot more difficult to connect with the benefits of resisting them. Therefore, we suggest first identifying these benefits when you're feeling relatively calm. Then, the next time you're angry, you can just read the list to increase your motivation to not act in ways you'll regret. Use exercise 7.3 to generate a list of the positive consequences of resisting urges to do something destructive.

Exercise 7.3 Positive Consequences of Not Acting on Urges to Engage in Destructive Behaviors

Think about the positive consequences of not acting on urges to engage in destructive behaviors. Try to identify as many benefits of resisting these urges as you can. Consider how not acting on these urges would impact your relationships, job, emotional health, physical health, and overall well-being.

RELATIONSHIP CONSEQUENCES

1. _____

2. _____

3. _____

4. _____

5. _____

JOB OR SCHOOL CONSEQUENCES

1. _____

2. _____

3. _____

4. _____

5. _____

EMOTIONAL HEALTH CONSEQUENCES

1. _____
2. _____
3. _____
4. _____
5. _____

PHYSICAL HEALTH CONSEQUENCES

1. _____
2. _____
3. _____
4. _____
5. _____

OTHER CONSEQUENCES

1. _____
2. _____
3. _____
4. _____
5. _____

STOP AND TAKE A STEP BACK

Although leaving the situation when you're really angry is a very useful skill, there will be times when it won't be possible to do so, or when leaving a situation has its own downsides. You may be in a moving car with someone else, or on a plane, or in an important meeting at work, or with young children who need constant supervision. When you can't physically leave the situation, one of the most effective ways to avoid making things worse is to simply stop and take a step back from the situation so you can catch your breath and figure out what to do next (Linehan 2015). There are five steps to follow to practice this skill:

1. Stop what you're doing. Don't make a move. Don't open your mouth. Just stop in your tracks.

2. Take a moment to center yourself. Allow yourself a brief pause. Take a deep breath. Count to ten in your mind. Or try some of the skills for keeping your mind busy that we described earlier.

3. Take a step back from the situation and notice what you're experiencing. Apply the mindfulness skill of attending to and objectively labeling your experience to get a better understanding of what is happening.

4. Think through the consequences of reacting out of anger and doing something destructive versus choosing to not act on anger urges and responding more effectively instead. Review your lists from exercises 7.2 and 7.3 on the negative consequences of acting on anger urges and the positive consequences of not acting on these urges.

5. Choose how to proceed. Think about what will be most effective in the long term. If your anger is getting in the way of thinking clearly, use the distraction skills from this chapter to distract yourself and give your anger time to pass. Continue to refrain from acting until you are able to leave the situation or your anger subsides.

The next time you're experiencing anger and believe you're at risk of doing something you'll regret, try this skill. You'll be amazed at how powerful just stopping in your tracks and taking a step back can be. Although pausing may only buy you a few minutes between having an action urge and acting on it, this can be enough time to connect with the downsides of acting on these urges and make a different choice.

Moving Forward

In this chapter, we focused on skills you can use to avoid making things worse when you're angry. Even though anger can be an incredibly helpful emotion, a lot of the action urges that go along with anger put people at risk of doing or saying things they'll later regret. The simple yet powerful skills in this chapter will help you avoid adding more stress and turmoil to an already difficult and painful situation. Leaving the situation that angered you and focusing your attention on something else can give your anger a chance to subside. Leaving the situation also gives you the opportunity to figure out how to respond most effectively. Even if you aren't able to physically leave an anger-provoking situation, you can still take a mental time-out by pausing, taking a step back, and thinking through the consequences of your behaviors before you act.

The skills in this chapter are all about damage control, but effectively managing anger involves a lot more than just avoiding harmful behaviors; it also involves learning how to regulate anger and reduce its intensity. Skills for reducing intense anger by modifying the physical sensations that go along with anger are the focus of the next chapter.

CHAPTER 8

Cooling the Flames of Anger by Reducing Its Physical Sensations

Because emotions are made up of three different components, one way to turn down the volume of an emotion is to modify these components. Modifying the physical sensations or thoughts that go along with an emotion or acting opposite an emotion's action urges are all skills for changing the experience of an emotion. An emotion of fear isn't the same if you don't have a racing heart, butterflies in your stomach, and muscle tension. Take these sensations away and the fear is going to be less intense. In the same way, if you alter the physical sensations or thoughts that go along with anger, you'll probably feel less angry and your anger will begin to subside. In later chapters we discuss skills for regulating anger by modifying the thoughts and action urges that go along with anger. This chapter is about modifying the physical sensations associated with anger.

As discussed in chapter 4, most of the physical sensations that go along with anger involve arousal and activation. When you experience anger, you get a surge of adrenaline, which is reflected in the way your body responds to this emotion: your heart races, your body tenses, your breathing becomes shallow, your face flushes, you sweat, and you feel a surge of energy. Reducing these sensations by slowing and deepening your breathing, reducing muscle tension, lowering your heart rate, cooling down your body, and releasing energy will help you regulate your anger.

DEEP BREATHING

Deep breathing is one of the most useful skills for reducing several of the physical sensations associated with anger (Linehan 1993b, 2015). Not only does this skill target the shallow breathing that often accompanies anger, it also reduces muscle tension and lowers your heart rate. The key is to learn how to breathe properly—in a way that reduces arousal.

So how do you know if you're breathing properly? Take a few minutes to practice breathing in and out slowly. Notice the parts of your body that move as you breathe, paying particular attention to the parts of your body that move in and out or up and down. If you are breathing properly, your belly should expand when you breathe in and contract when you breathe out. If this is the case, you are using your diaphragm (the big muscle below your stomach) to breathe, which is what you want. On the other hand, if your shoulders move up and down as you breathe, you're probably not breathing properly, and you may even be putting yourself at risk for more intense feelings of anger. When you use your chest and shoulders to breathe, your lungs don't have enough room to expand, which results in short and shallow breaths—the very sensations we are working to reduce!

Training yourself to use your diaphragm to breathe will help you take deeper, slower breaths. Not only will deep, slow breathing make your breathing less shallow, breathing out slowly can slow down your heart rate and reduce muscle tension. Exercise 8.1 (Gratz and Chapman 2009) provides simple step-by-step instructions for learning how to breathe deeply. Try it out and see how it works!

Exercise 8.1   Learning How to Breathe Deeply

The first few times you practice this exercise, choose a time when you already feel relaxed. It's easier to learn the basic techniques of deep breathing when you're not stressed-out.

1. Find a comfortable and quiet place. Sit up in a chair so that your back is straight.

2. Close your eyes.

3. Put the palm of one hand on your stomach and the palm of the other hand on your chest across your breastbone.

4. Breathe in and out as you normally do. Which hand moves the most when you breathe? If the hand on your chest moves and the one on your belly doesn't, this means that you're not breathing with your diaphragm.

5. To correct this, deliberately push your belly out when you breathe in and let your belly fall when you breathe out. It may feel slightly unnatural at first, but this feeling will go away very quickly with practice.

6. Continue to breathe in and out. Try to lengthen your breaths. Slowly count to five as you breathe in and again when you breathe out. Breathing in through your nose and exhaling through your mouth may help you take deeper breaths.

7. Practice this breathing exercise a couple of times a day. The more you practice, the more it will become a habit.

Once you've practiced deep breathing a few times, it's time to try it out when you feel angry. Although deep breathing is a useful skill for managing stress and reducing vulnerability to intense anger (not to mention supplying your brain with the oxygen it needs to function at its best!), the focus of this chapter is reducing the physical sensations that go along with anger. And that means using this skill when you're angry.

One nice thing about this particular skill is that you can use it any time or any place. You can use it at work, at home, when you're alone, or when you're with other people. There isn't a time when deep breathing isn't possible. Unlike other skills that require you to plan ahead and bring something with you, your breath is always there! So the next time you notice your anger intensifying, focus your attention on taking deeper breaths and using your diaphragm to breathe. Even though changing your breathing may seem simple, it can have a profound effect on your anger.

SLOWING YOUR BREATHING

Slowing your breathing is a very similar skill that may be easier to use in the moment, especially if you aren't used to breathing with your diaphragm. Instead of focusing on your belly and breathing more deeply, all this skill requires is breathing out more slowly than you breathe in and gradually lengthening your out-breath. For example, if your breathing is rapid and your out-breath lasts only one second, focus on slowing your out-breath to three seconds, and then four seconds, and then five seconds, and so on. The goal is to increase the length of your out-breath one to two seconds with each breath until you are breathing about six to eight breaths per minute. An added benefit of this skill is that counting the length of each out-breath can help distract you from whatever made you angry by focusing your mind on something else.

PROGRESSIVE MUSCLE RELAXATION

Progressive muscle relaxation (PMR) involves tensing and then relaxing the various muscles in your body. Since the goal of this skill is to relax your muscles, it's going to be most helpful for reducing the muscle tension that goes along with anger. However, you might also find that it slows down your heart rate as well.

The reason this skill involves tensing your muscles before you relax them is that it can be quite difficult to relax muscles on command. Asking people to just relax tense muscles doesn't tend to work. However, if you tense your muscles first, you can relax them more easily, and also notice the difference between the tense and relaxed states. Noticing this difference will help you recognize muscle tension earlier. Exercise 8.2 (Gratz and Chapman 2009) describes how to practice PMR.

Exercise 8.2 Simple Steps for Practicing Progressive Muscle Relaxation

1. Find a quiet place where you won't be disturbed and get into a comfortable position. You can practice this exercise lying down, sitting up, or even standing up, but you might find that lying down works best.

2. Choose a part of your body to start the exercise. Many people find it helpful to start with the top of their head or the tips of their toes.

3. Bring your full attention to that part of your body. If you started with your forearms, imagine that your whole brain is being drawn to your forearms. Make fists with your hands and squeeze to about 75 to 80 percent of your maximum strength, and then hold them tense for about five to ten seconds.

4. Release your fists and relax your muscles. Notice the difference between how they felt when they were tense and how they feel now. Notice any sensations that are present, such as sensations of relaxation or warmth.

5. Repeat this process again, first tensing the muscles in your forearms, then holding that tension for five to ten seconds, and then relaxing the muscles.

6. Now focus your attention on another area of your body. For instance, bring your attention to your lower legs and clench your calf muscles tightly. Hold this tension for five to ten seconds and then relax your calf muscles. Repeat this process again and notice any differences in sensations between the tense and relaxed muscles.

7. Continue going through different muscle groups in your body. Each time, tense your muscles to about 75 to 80 percent of your maximum strength, hold for about five to ten seconds, and then relax your muscles, focusing on the differences you feel.

Depending on how much time you have, you can practice PMR for five to twenty-five minutes. Even doing it for only five minutes can make a difference in how you feel.

As with the breathing skills, the goal is to be able to use PMR when you're feeling angry. Don't get us wrong—using PMR to relax your body any time you notice tension can decrease stress and reduce your vulnerability to intense emotions in general. However, if you're using this skill to regulate anger, it's best to use it when you're angry.

The fact that your body is always with you means that this is another skill you can use anywhere, but how you use it will depend on the situation you're in. If you're by yourself in your home or office and have a few minutes, you can practice this skill exactly as described in exercise 8.2. If you're driving, focus on tensing and relaxing any muscles you aren't using to drive. Although we recommend that you avoid focusing on your right foot and leg so you don't accidentally hit the gas pedal, there are many other areas of your body you can focus on while driving. For example, focusing on your shoulders and neck might be particularly helpful, as these are often the first muscles to become tense in the car.

You can even use this skill if you're out in public or with other people. You may not be able to focus on all of your muscles, but there are many you can tense and relax without anyone knowing. You might look silly if you tensed and relaxed the muscles in your face, but we doubt anyone would notice if you tensed and relaxed the muscles in your legs, back, shoulders, or neck. You could also use the strategies for excusing yourself from a situation that we discussed in chapter 7 so you can practice PMR in private. Even if you can only get away for one minute, you can use a version of this skill by tensing and relaxing all of your muscles at once. Doing so only takes a moment, but it can leave your body feeling more relaxed.

LOWERING YOUR BODY TEMPERATURE

In addition to being an arousing and energizing emotion, you can think of anger as a "hot" emotion. Think about common expressions used to describe anger, such as "boiling over," "steamed up," "blood boiling," and the "flames of anger," to name just a few. One reason phrases such as this exist is because your body does actually heat up when you experience anger. Therefore, lowering your body temperature is one strategy for reducing the physical component of anger (Linehan 2015). Doing so sends a message to your brain that your anger is becoming less intense. There are a number of different ways to lower your body temperature:

- Take a very cold shower.

- Hold an ice pack or ice cubes on your cheeks, wrists, or the back of your neck.

- Hold your breath and dunk your face in a bowl of cold water.

- Sit in a very cold bath.

If you're at home when you're feeling angry, using these strategies can be fairly simple and straightforward. As long as you have access to your kitchen and bathroom, you probably have everything you need to use these skills. And even if you aren't able to use all of these skills when you're at work, school, or in the presence of others, there are a number of ways you can use some of them in public. For example, a partially frozen drink in a plastic bottle can replace an ice pack. If you expect a particular situation to be anger provoking, bring a drink with a lot of ice in it so you can hold it against your wrists. And in a pinch, going to the bathroom and running very cold water on your wrists and arms is a great way to lower your body temperature.

RELEASING THE ENERGY ASSOCIATED WITH ANGER

Because many of the physical sensations associated with anger involve increases in energy and arousal, one way to regulate anger and reduce its intensity is to engage in activities that release this energy (Linehan 2015). It's hard to experience intense anger if your body is exhausted, so anything you can do to release the energy associated with anger is going to reduce its intensity and help it pass. There are many ways to release the energy associated with anger.

- **Do intense physical exercise.** Run as hard and fast as you can until you tire yourself out. Do push-ups or pull-ups until your arms are shaking and you can't do any more. Go to the gym and do an intense workout. Go on a long hike of at least moderate difficulty. Do jumping jacks, squats, lunges, or some other activity that quickly engages your legs, which have the largest muscles in your body. The goal is to engage in exercise that's intense for you. Although this will vary depending on your age and overall physical health, anything that gets your heart pounding and your muscles working at full capacity will do.

- **Do some other intense physical activity.** Clean your entire house or apartment from top to bottom, including vacuuming, scrubbing floors, and cleaning windows. Shovel snow or mow your lawn. Go to the batting cage and hit balls until your arms are tired. Walk up and down long flights of stairs. Focus on any activity that takes a lot of energy and wears you out.

As you probably noticed, some of these skills require more time, specialized equipment or locations, or the help of Mother Nature than many of the other skills we've discussed in this chapter. Unless you live in a particularly cold and snowy place, you won't be able to shovel snow any time you get angry. Likewise, going to the gym isn't always possible. However, that doesn't mean there aren't things you can do to release the energy associated with anger. You just need to be creative. For example, if you're at work and can't take a break to go outside, try walking up and down a flight of stairs or doing lunges or squats in your office, the bathroom, or a stairwell. As long as you can find some privacy, it's possible to run in place almost anywhere.

As you're doing these activities, it's also important to make sure you're not ruminating about what made you angry or getting caught up in angry thoughts. Doing an intense physical activity while simultaneously ruminating about what made you angry will prevent this skill from working and may even make your anger more intense. Therefore, as you engage in these physical activities, be sure to focus all of your attention on the activity itself.

PRACTICING THE SKILLS

Now that you've learned a number of different skills for reducing the physical sensations of anger, it's time to try them out and see how they work. You may want to begin by reviewing exercise 4.3 to see which of the physical sensations we focused on in this chapter are most relevant for you. If most of the sensations you marked involve tightness or tension, you may find it helpful to start with PMR or some of the activities for releasing energy. On the other hand, if you marked a lot of sensations related to feeling hot, flushed, or sweaty, you may want to focus on lowering your body temperature. Use exercise 8.3 to track your use of these skills and figure out which work best for you.

Exercise 8.3   Skills for Reducing the Physical Sensations of Anger

To use this exercise, first rate the intensity of your anger on a scale of 0 (no anger at all) to 10 (the most intense anger ever) in the "Anger Before" column. Then try one of the skills listed in the left-hand column. Immediately after using a skill, rate your anger again in the "Anger After" column. Use this rating to determine which skills work best for you.

Skill	Anger Before (0 to 10)	Anger After (0 to 10)
Deep breathing		
Slowing your breathing		
Progressive muscle relaxation		
Lowering your body temperature		
Take a very cold shower.		
Hold an ice pack or ice cubes on your cheeks, neck, or wrists.		
Dunk your face in a bowl of cold water.		
Sit in a very cold bath.		
Releasing the energy associated with anger		
Intense physical exercise (list the activities you tried here).		

Other intense physical activity (list the activities you tried here).		

Comments: Include any comments on what you tried, whether or not it worked for you, and what you might do the next time you want to reduce the physical sensations that go along with anger.

Moving Forward

In this chapter, we described skills you can use to reduce the physical sensations of anger, including skills for reducing muscle tension, deepening and slowing breathing, lowering body temperature, and releasing the energy associated with anger. The next chapter focuses on the cognitive component of anger and describes skills for regulating anger by modifying anger-related thoughts or how you respond to those thoughts.

CHAPTER 9

Managing Angry Thoughts

As we discussed in the last chapter, one way to regulate an emotion is to modify one of its three components. In this chapter we focus on the cognitive component of anger and describe several skills you can use to manage the thoughts that accompany anger.

ANGER AND THOUGHTS HAVE A BACK-AND-FORTH RELATIONSHIP

As we discussed in chapters 1 and 4, certain types of thinking go hand in hand with anger, including judgmental thoughts, rumination, and extreme or hostile thoughts. Sometimes these thoughts are the primary fuel for anger. At other times, anger might be the primary fuel for these thoughts. Thoughts and emotions have this back-and-forth relationship, in which emotions can lead to thoughts and thoughts can lead to emotions. In fact, all three parts of the anger system (cognitive, behavioral, and physical) are related.

This back-and-forth between thoughts and emotions can escalate anger. You have probably noticed this. Something happens, you start to get angry, and then you have all sorts of negative thoughts about the situation. These thoughts increase your anger, leading to even more negative or extreme thoughts. This back-and-forth can become a difficult and vicious cycle.

IDENTIFYING ANGER-RELATED THINKING

The first step in dealing with any kind of thinking pattern is to identify it. In order to identify your thoughts, you have to be able to step back and notice what is going through your mind. Mindfully attending to your thoughts (chapters 4 and 6) will help you do this. Once you recognize thinking patterns that lead you astray, you'll be in a better position to manage them before they contribute to the vicious cycle of anger.

Knowing what types of thinking patterns to watch out for can make it easier to notice when you're engaging in anger-related thinking. We discuss some of the most common patterns below.

Rumination

Rumination (see also chapter 1) involves repetitively thinking about and focusing on the problem that is making you angry (Nolen-Hoeksema 1991). When you ruminate, you might feel like you're doing something productive because you're focusing on your problems. Rumination, however, doesn't solve your problems, and it almost always makes anger worse. There are many signs that you might be ruminating (some taken from Peled and Moretti 2007):

- Asking yourself why things are the way they are (for example, *Why is this happening? Why am I so upset?*)

- Wondering what's wrong with yourself for feeling or thinking the way you do

- Thinking that whatever problem you're stressed or angry about always happens to you

- Asking yourself why this kind of thing keeps happening to you

- Thinking over and over about whatever you're angry about

- Having a hard time stopping yourself from thinking about something

- Thinking and rethinking until you feel more angry

- Feeling burned-out, tired, or exhausted from thinking about why you're angry

Judgmental Thinking

Judgmental thinking is all about categorizing a situation, yourself, another person, or a thing as good or bad or right or wrong. And when it comes to anger, judgments are almost always about something being bad. As we mentioned in chapter 1, judging is a normal human activity. We all do it. The challenge is to identify when you're judging and to find a way to avoid letting it intensify your anger or other emotions. There are many signs that you might be judging:

- Having thoughts that things shouldn't be the way they are

- Thinking that something should never have happened

- Thinking that another person, thing, situation, or event is *bad*, *wrong*, *unfair*, *unjust*, or *evil*

- Describing yourself or others with negative labels, such as "selfish," "rude," or "obnoxious"

Making Assumptions

As is true with judging, it's normal to make assumptions about the intentions of other people. It's human nature to try to figure out why people do the things they do. The problem is that you can't really know their intentions unless they tell you. And assuming negative intentions is a recipe for anger and suspicion. Examples include thinking that the person driving slowly in front of you is doing so to ruin your day, thinking that a loved one who sounded irritable was intentionally trying to hurt your feelings, or thinking that someone is trying to manipulate you or take advantage of you. Thinking that others are out to harm you can make you feel the need to defend or protect yourself, and this can lead to anger as well. If you answer yes to some of the questions below, you are making assumptions, and this thinking pattern could be fueling your anger:

- Do you make a lot of guesses about why people do the things they do, particularly when you're annoyed?

- Do these guesses often include negative thoughts about these people?

- Do you often think people are doing upsetting things on purpose?

- When someone makes a mistake or does something that upsets you, do you assume that person is doing it in order to upset you?

- Do you tend to think that the actions of other people have something to do with you?

- Do you view others as uncaring, mean, selfish, or out for themselves?

Blaming Yourself or Others

Blaming is exactly what it sounds like: thinking that you, someone, or something is responsible for a negative event. When you blame others, they become the target of your anger. Often, the more you think about how they are to blame, the angrier you feel. Similarly, if you think you messed up somehow or did the wrong thing, you're probably going to feel angry with yourself or even ashamed.

Another problem with blaming is that fault rarely lies with one person or event. Let's say the weatherperson reports that it's going to be sunny, so you decide to go out without a raincoat and then get caught in a downpour. Frustrated, you curse and blame the weatherperson for your discomfort. You might think that it's the weatherperson's fault that you got wet. People with anger-management problems often blame others for their blowups. Have you ever had a heated argument or discussion in which it felt like someone was really pressing your buttons, and then you blew up and yelled at the person? During this altercation, or afterward, you might have blamed this person for your blowup.

Blaming yourself or others is a relatively simple thinking pattern to identify. If you think that you or someone else is to blame for whatever is upsetting you, you're likely blaming.

Extreme or Absolute Thinking

Much like judging, *extreme* or *absolute thinking* involves categorizing things as either right or wrong, good or bad, perfect or horrible, and so on. This type of thinking is also called *dichotomous* or *black-and-white thinking*. People are particularly prone to engaging in extreme or absolute thinking when they're angry because anger gives us tunnel vision. When you're angry, it's difficult to consider all sides of a situation or argument; you tend to get stuck thinking about only your side. You might think that you're completely right and the person you're dealing with is completely wrong. Most situations and arguments, however, are not black and white. Even in the most heated of arguments, there is probably truth to both sides. There are many signs that you're engaging in absolute or extreme thinking:

- Having the words "always" or "never" go through your mind

- Thinking of yourself or others as either a success or a failure but nothing in between

- Thinking that something or someone is plain wrong

- Being unable to put yourself in the other person's shoes

- Using extreme words like "horrible" or "awful"

MINDFULLY ATTENDING TO AND LETTING GO OF YOUR THOUGHTS

Whichever form of anger-related thinking you're dealing with, mindfully attending to and letting go of your thoughts can be a very helpful skill. We understand that this might seem a little strange. If your thoughts increase your anger, why would you want to pay more attention to them? As surprising at it may seem, paying attention to your thoughts with mindfulness actually takes away some of their power over you and makes you less likely to get caught up in them.

Mindfully attending to your thoughts and letting go of them can also help you learn that you can choose whether or not to act on your thoughts. Just because you think something doesn't mean you have to do it. If someone is rude to you, and you feel hurt and frustrated, you might think about being rude in return. That's perfectly understandable; many people think that way. Just because that thought rolls through your mind, however, doesn't mean you have to act on it. In fact, acting on it might be ineffective. For example, let's say your boss is rude to you. The next day you find out that she was irritable and upset because her husband had just left her. Had you returned the rudeness in kind, not only would you have made your situation worse, but you would have hurt someone who's already suffering.

The good news is the more you practice stepping back and being mindful of your thoughts, the easier it becomes to choose which thoughts to act on and which ones to let go of. As a result, you will take some of the power out of your anger-related thoughts and find that your behavior is more effective in the long run. Many people find this exercise helpful for mindfully attending to and letting go of thoughts:

- Sit in a relaxed position and close your eyes.

- Take a few slow, deep breaths until you feel relaxed and centered.

- Bring your attention to the thoughts going through your mind. Simply shine the spotlight of your attention on them. It's okay if you don't notice any thoughts at first; this is a common experience. Some people find that as soon as they focus on their thoughts, the thoughts disappear. Don't worry; they're bound to come back.

- Whatever thought goes through your mind, put it in one of three categories. If you're thinking about the past, then say to yourself, *This is a thought about the past.* If you're thinking about right now, then say to yourself, *This is a thought about the present.* And if you're thinking about the future, then say to yourself, *This is a thought about the future.* Your job is to pay attention to each thought that goes through your mind and to put it into one of these categories.

- For example, if you think about a meal you had yesterday, put that thought in the past category. If you think about a twinge of pain in your foot, put that thought in the present category. If you think about something that is coming up tomorrow or next week, put that thought in the future category.

- Avoid being overly concerned about whether you are putting thoughts in the correct categories. Choosing the perfect category is not the point of the exercise; rather, it's to practice experiencing your thoughts in a different way instead of getting wrapped up in them.

- Try this exercise for five to ten minutes. It can be helpful to set a timer so you know when the time is up.

Sometimes people feel much more relaxed after doing this exercise. This is not always the case, especially if the thoughts that went through their mind were troubling or upsetting. Don't worry if this exercise isn't relaxing or calming. The goal is to practice taking a step back from whatever thoughts are present in your mind.

Another exercise that can help you practice mindfully attending to and letting go of your thoughts involves imagery and visualization:

- Instead of categorizing your thoughts, imagine you are sitting on the side of a lovely grassy hill looking down at a train slowly going by.

- Think of each thought that goes through your mind as one of the cars of the train.

- Allow the train to simply go by, and let go of whatever thoughts you are experiencing.

- Resist the urge to jump on the train. Instead, remain firmly planted on the grassy hillside watching your thoughts go by.

These are just a couple of different ways to practice mindfully attending to and letting go of your thoughts. Choose the exercise that works best for you, and feel free to modify it as needed. It doesn't matter which exercise you use as long as you are able to take a step back from your thoughts and not get caught up in them. The types of thoughts you have also don't matter. Mindfully attending to and letting go of your thoughts is a helpful skill for managing any of the thinking patterns we described earlier. In fact, you can even practice it with pleasant thoughts.

Although this skill is very effective, in the heat of the moment, when you're feeling very angry, you probably won't want to simply let your thoughts come and go. In fact, you'll probably be really attached to them. Because it can be difficult to use this skill when you're angry, we recommend that you practice mindfulness exercises regularly. Each time you practice, you are teaching your mind how to notice and let go of thoughts. And the more you practice, the easier it will be to mindfully attend to and let go of thoughts when you're frustrated and angry.

LETTING GO OF JUDGMENTS AND ASSUMPTIONS

Another helpful strategy for managing angry thoughts involves letting go of judgments and assumptions about other people. You can also use this strategy to let go of extreme, absolute, or blaming thoughts (as shown in a couple of examples below). There are three key steps to letting go of judgments and assumptions.

1. Mindfully Attend To and Let Go Of Your Thoughts

We discussed this skill in detail above. In short, it involves stepping back and noticing the thoughts going through your mind without getting wrapped up in them.

2. Identify Judgments and Assumptions

We provided guidance above on how to notice when you're judging or making assumptions. You first need to identify judgments or assumptions before you can do anything about them. You're probably judging if you think things shouldn't be the way they are or that something is good or bad or wrong or right. You're probably making assumptions if you're thinking about the feelings, thoughts, or intentions of others. If you notice that you're judging, say to yourself, *This is a judgment.* If you notice that you're making assumptions, say to yourself, *This is an assumption.*

You might consider keeping track of your judgments and assumptions on a piece of paper, on your smartphone, or in some other way. Some people use a golf score counter or similar device, which they click whenever they make an assumption or have a judgmental thought. If you keep track, you might be quite surprised by how many assumptions and judgments go through your mind each day.

3. Objectively Label Your Experiences

After you've practiced identifying judgments and assumptions, it's time to start practicing strategies to let go of them. As we've mentioned throughout this book, objectively labeling your experiences involves simply describing the facts (Linehan 1993b, 2015). The idea is to let go of judgments and assumptions and to simply describe what is going on as if you're a fly on the wall or a video camera that can talk. As far as we know, flies and video cameras are not biased.

To get your feet wet with objectively labeling your experiences, think about a recent time when somebody moderately annoyed you. Don't focus on an experience that left you enraged. Using exercise 9.1, describe that person's behavior and the situation. Include all negative judgments and assumptions that come to mind. Let it rip—describe the experience as you would have to a friend at the time.

Exercise 9.1   Your Description, Including Judgments and Assumptions

Example: Paul was such a jerk last night when I came home. He was just sitting around, all lazy, watching television and drinking beer with his friends. He had the gall to ask me if I brought home dinner. The kitchen was a total mess. He's such a lazy slob. He's just a user who is taking advantage of me. (Annoyance rating: 8/10)

Circle all of the judgments, assumptions, and extreme or absolute statements you made in exercise 9.1. Circle anything that is not a fact—anything that you did not directly experience. Judgments in our example include "jerk," "lazy," and "user." "Total mess" is an extreme statement. "Taking advantage of me" could be an assumption. In your own example, look for these types of statements. Circle judgment words like "good," "bad," "selfish," "rude," and "mean." Also, circle words like "should," because one type of judging involves thinking that you, others, and situations *should* be different. Once you've circled all of the words and phrases that are not strictly the facts, use exercise 9.2 to rewrite your description using only facts about what happened. Imagine that you are in court, and you are not allowed to include conjecture, assumptions, guesses, hunches, or judgments.

Exercise 9.2 Your Nonjudgmental Description of the Facts

Example: When I came home last night, Paul was watching television and drinking beer with his friends. In the kitchen, there were several unwashed dishes on the counter. Paul said he was hungry and asked if I had brought dinner home. I felt really frustrated when I saw him sitting and relaxing. I had a long day at work, and I felt annoyed when he asked for dinner. (Annoyance rating: 6/10)

Now read both of your descriptions. On a scale from 0 (not annoyed at all) to 10 (really annoyed), rate how annoyed you feel when you read each one. You might find both descriptions equally annoying, but some people feel less annoyed when they read the more factual description. Objectively labeling and describing your experience will not get rid of anger or annoyance, but it will probably take the edge off. Once you have practiced objectively labeling and describing some past experiences, try this skill out in your daily life when you notice assumptions, judgments, or other anger-provoking thoughts. These thoughts are an opportunity to practice this new way of thinking—sticking like glue to the facts rather than adding things that make you angrier.

THINKING FLEXIBLY

Thinking flexibly can be particularly helpful when you find yourself interpreting the actions of others. As we've discussed, anger can give you tunnel vision. When you're angry, you have a hard time seeing all sides of an issue, understanding other perspectives, and considering alternative ways of thinking about things. Thinking flexibly is all about being able to come up with different ways to see the same thing.

Table 9.1 offers different possible interpretations for the same situation. After you read through what we came up with, use exercise 9.3 to describe a recent situation in which someone annoyed you. Next, write down the interpretations you had about why the person did what she or he did. Finally, write down all of the *alternative* interpretations you can come up with to explain that person's behavior. Let your brain freely come up with alternative interpretations. Don't worry about how silly or realistic they are; just write them down as soon as they occur to you. Being right is not the goal here; stretching your thinking muscles and getting used to thinking flexibly and creatively about situations that make you angry is. With practice, you might find that you're much less likely to get locked into interpretations and assumptions that make you even angrier. You'll be more able to open your mind to the other possibilities. When this happens, your anger will probably start to feel more manageable. Some of these steps come from the DBT skill of checking the facts (Linehan 2015).

Table 9.1   Interpretations and Alternative Interpretations

Situation

When I was putting cream in my coffee at a local coffee shop, I bumped into John, an old friend I hadn't seen for about three years. He looked at me, frowned, and said, "Oh, it's you."

Interpretation

He doesn't like me and he didn't want to see me.

Alternative interpretations

He was really tired.

He had a bad day and was upset.

He had bad news to share with me.

He was surprised to see me.

He was caught off guard and didn't know what to say.

He has poor social skills.

His brain was addled from too much coffee.

He is diabetic, and he was experiencing high blood sugar from eating too many pastries. Seeing me confused him.

Exercise 9.3 Interpretations and Alternative Interpretations for Your Own Experience

Situation

Interpretation

Alternative interpretations

Moving Forward

In this chapter, we reviewed several common thinking patterns that go along with anger. These include rumination, judgmental thinking, making assumptions, blaming yourself or others, and extreme or absolute thinking. Some key skills to help you free yourself from the negative effects of these thinking patterns include mindfully attending to and letting go of your thoughts, letting go of judgments and assumptions, and thinking flexibly. As you become more aware of your own thinking patterns and get more practice with these skills, you will be able to step out of the vicious cycle of thoughts inflaming anger and vice versa. In the next chapter, we address ways to use interpersonal skills to communicate effectively when you're angry.

CHAPTER 10

Using Opposite Action
to Reduce Anger

In chapters 8 and 9, we described skills for regulating anger by modifying the physical sensations (physical component) and thoughts (cognitive component) that go along with anger. This chapter focuses on changing the behavioral component, which involves the actions that go along with anger. One of the most effective ways to deal with anger is to do the opposite of what your action urges are telling you to do. This skill is called *opposite action* (Linehan 1993b, 2015).

WHAT IS OPPOSITE ACTION?

In chapters 6 and 7, we showed you ways to avoid acting on your urges. Opposite action is slightly different in that it involves actively doing the opposite of what those urges are telling you to do.

Many people suffer from *phobias*, which are unrealistic fears of certain situations or objects. One of the best treatments for different phobias is called *exposure therapy*. This treatment involves exposing clients to whatever they're afraid of. For someone with a phobia about spiders, exposure therapy involves looking at, being in the same room as, and even touching nonpoisonous spiders. The idea is that through contact with safe spiders, in which nothing bad actually happens, the brain will learn that spiders are not dangerous and the client's fear will diminish. The same general idea applies to all sorts of fears, including being with other people, public speaking, exposure to heights, and being in enclosed spaces, among others. In essence, exposure therapy involves opposite action.

Opposite action also works quite well for treating depression. One of the best treatments for depression, particularly severe depression, is called *behavioral activation* (Cuijpers, Van Straten, and Warmerdam 2007; Mazzucchelli, Kane, and Rees 2009), which involves actively engaging in activities you have been (or feel like) avoiding. Just as approaching a spider is the last thing someone with a spider phobia wants to do, getting out of bed, leaving home, being active, and seeing other people are often the last things someone with depression wants to do. As it turns out, the more that people engage in doing the opposite of what they feel like doing (the opposite of their action urges), the more free they become from depression.

OPPOSITE ACTION FOR ANGER

So how does opposite action apply to anger? As Dr. Marsha Linehan says in her video *Opposite Action: Changing Emotions You Want to Change*, emotions seem to "love themselves." What she means is that an emotion makes you feel like doing things to keep the emotion around. For example, when you're angry and you yell or act in an aggressive manner, you are adding fuel to your anger, keeping it alive.

Have you ever noticed that your anger intensifies when you act in an angry way? People often say that yelling helps them blow off steam. But actively yelling is like barreling uncontrollably down a hill in a car and pressing on the gas instead of hitting the brakes. As you're yelling, your nervous system revs up, intensifying feelings of anger. Instead of blowing off steam, you're actually increasing your agitation. Acting on your urges when you are angry, such as yelling, creates a vicious cycle that can lead to disastrous consequences.

There is a way to break this vicious cycle—by changing your actions. Opposite action breaks the cycle of anger by directly modifying anger's behavioral component. By doing the opposite of your angry urges, you can reduce your anger and deal with it effectively, just as slowing down and gently applying the brakes can help you get a car under control. If you practice opposite action, you may discover that you can avoid consequences that make you angrier, such as conflict with other people, or lead to other negative emotions, such as guilt, shame, and sadness.

STEPS FOR OPPOSITE ACTION

Although the skill of opposite action might seem complicated at first, with practice it will start to feel more natural. With a lot of practice, you might find yourself using opposite action automatically, without much thought or effort. There are five key steps to practicing opposite action.

1. Identify What Emotion You Are Experiencing

The first and most important step is to figure out what emotion you are feeling. You can use the skills in chapter 4 to help you figure out exactly what you might be feeling and how to label the emotion accurately. Although opposite action works for many emotions, this book focuses on anger, so we're going to assume you have identified your emotion as anger or a related emotion, such as annoyance, irritation, or frustration.

2. Determine If Your Anger Is Effective

Generally, opposite action is useful when anger is not effective. Anger is effective when it motivates you to do things that improve your situation. For example, if the way a loved one treats you makes you frustrated or angry, your anger might motivate you to change or improve the relationship. Perhaps you decide to sit the person down for a heart-to-heart conversation. On the other hand, anger can be ineffective when it lasts for a long time, is extremely intense, or leads to actions that make your situation worse. For example, you yell at your relative and damage an already fragile relationship. If you answer yes to any of the following questions, your anger may be ineffective:

- Am I a lot more angry about this than I'd like to be?

- Is anger lasting a long time and interfering with my activities or everyday life?

- Is anger making me want to do things that would make my situation worse?

- Is anger getting in the way of my goals and relationships?

3. Describe Your Action Urges

An action urge is what your anger makes you feel like doing. Describing your action urges is an important step, because the skill of opposite action involves doing the opposite of what these action urges are telling you to do. It might helpful to review exercise 4.5 to identify your action urges. Once you have a clear idea of what they are, it will be much easier to figure out how to do the opposite.

4. Choose an Opposite Action

The next step is to figure out what opposite action to use. Although what you actually feel like doing when you're angry will determine which one you choose, there are a few common opposite actions that work in most situations.

Gracefully leave the situation. Because the urges to lash out or confront others often go with anger, an effective opposite action is to leave the situation that is making you angry (Linehan 1993b, 2015). (We discussed the same strategy in chapter 7, in which we reviewed skills you can use to avoid making things worse.) For example, if you have the urge to yell at someone, the opposite action is to gracefully leave the situation. There are many different ways to do this:

- If you're at a party and feeling angry with one of the guests, you could hang out in rooms or areas of the house this person isn't in, excuse yourself if this person enters a room you're in, or gracefully avoid conversations or other interactions with this person.

- If you're having a heated discussion or argument with someone and your anger is making it hard for you to communicate effectively, you could politely ask to continue the discussion later, when you are calmer.

- If you're feeling angry or frustrated with your roommates, partner, or children while at home, you could find a quiet room where you can read a book, watch television, or engage in a different distracting or soothing activity. Don't stomp off. Instead, leave quietly or explain that you need a breather ("I need some time alone").

- If a conversation is starting to make you angry or frustrated, you could gently change the topic by asking a question or making a statement about something else. You could also ask if it would be okay to talk about something else for a while.

- If something on television is making you angry, such as an upsetting news story, you could temporarily change the channel.

Sometimes it's just not possible or reasonable to leave a situation. You can't always leave important meetings at work when your coworkers or boss say things that make you angry. You can't get out of your car when you're driving. But even if you can't physically get away from a situation, you can still avoid it by focusing your attention on something else.

• Sandra's Story

Sandra found herself really frustrated with some of the clients in her therapy group. She thought they were monopolizing the conversation and making irrelevant and off-topic comments, and she had urges to yell at them to shut up. To help Sandra avoid acting on these urges, her therapist suggested that she mentally distract herself when her anger became intense. When the clients began to talk in her therapy group, Sandra would appear courteous and alert while thinking about distracting topics, such as a trip she was looking forward to, her favorite television show, or her grocery list. She found that this brief mental escape reduced her anger and prevented her from saying something rude to her fellow group members.

Be compassionate and kind. Because the action urges that often accompany anger tell you to be hostile, aggressive, or confrontational, the opposite action is to be kind, gentle, and compassionate. It is very hard to feel compassion and anger at the same time. They're incompatible feelings—one cancels the other out. You've probably noticed this phenomenon. When you're really angry with someone, you're probably not thinking about how she or he feels because your anger cancels out your compassion. The good news is that compassion also cancels out anger.

The opposite action of being compassionate and kind involves changing both your behavior and your thinking. In terms of behavior, the opposite action often involves treating others with fairness and respect while being polite, kind, and thoughtful. The key to using this skill successfully, though, is to also change your attitude. Acting kind but continuing to judge the person who is upsetting you will probably make you more angry, make you feel fake, or make you feel untrue to your feelings (Linehan 2007). You need to be able to change how you think about the person internally so your attitude about the person matches your actions. There are a couple of strategies that will help you act with kindness and compassion with both mind and body.

- *Use mindfulness to let go of judgments.* In chapter 6 we discussed how mindfully attending to and objectively labeling your experiences can help you let go of thinking patterns that inflame anger. Use these skills to bring your full attention to the present moment. If you feel angry at someone you're interacting with, pay attention to that person. Listen mindfully and convey interest in what this person is saying. Let go of resentment and negative judgments about this person. If you throw your mind into the moment, angry thoughts will have a difficult time hijacking your mind and body.

- *Jump into the other person's shoes.* When we are angry, often we're only paying attention to our own perspective. Anger narrows our focus and attention so that we don't see the bigger picture. Instead, our attention becomes focused on whatever immediate goal we are trying to achieve, such as expressing our opinion, criticizing someone, or getting past barriers. You've probably noticed this. Perhaps you've said something harsh to a loved one, only to realize later on that what you said was very hurtful. In the heat of the moment, anger blinded you. You weren't paying attention to the effects your behavior was having on the other person. Instead of being completely focused on your own point of view, do the opposite: try to understand how the other person's point of view, thoughts, feelings, and reactions make sense (Linehan 2007). You don't have to agree with the other person's perspective or behavior, you just have to try to understand these things. It helps to ask yourself a few questions: *How do this person's thoughts and feelings make sense? What if I was in the same situation? What if I had the same life? How would I feel, think, and act?*

- *Use your body.* Anger is accompanied by changes in the body, such as with posture, voice tone, and demeanor. By applying the skill of opposite action to these changes, you can modify your behavior. For example, if you normally have a scowl on your face when you're angry, you could focus on having a pleasant or peaceful expression. If your voice gets louder when you're angry, you could speak very softly instead. If you get tense and clench your fists when you're angry, the opposite would be to relax your muscles and unclench your hands.

The following exercise illustrates how you can use the power of your body to influence anger.

- Start by thinking about a person or situation that recently made you angry. The first time you do this, it might be helpful to choose something that resulted in moderate anger, frustration, or irritation rather than intense rage.

- After about a minute has passed, sit back in a relaxed, open position. Relax your muscles and rest your hands palms up on your knees or the arms of the chair (if they are available).

- Make sure your facial muscles are relaxed, and then turn up the corners of your mouth until you have a half smile (Linehan 1993b, 2015). This is the kind of smile the Buddha has, or the *Mona Lisa*; it's not a huge grin but rather a slight smile of peace or serenity.

- Stay like this for two to three minutes.

- Afterward, describe your experiences on a piece of paper. What kinds of thoughts went through your mind? How did you feel physically? How angry were you?

Many people notice that their anger diminishes and doesn't last as long when they do this exercise and that angry thoughts are harder to focus on. Some people even notice that they feel some amount of warmth and compassion for the person they were angry with. If you notice similar things, you'll see how your body has a strong influence on how you feel, especially about a situation or person that made you angry.

The open posture and half smile also directly communicate to your brain that things are okay—that there is no danger. Remember how we talked about anger being part of the fight-flight-freeze response? In this way, anger is a strong ally when you are threatened. But what if you're not really being threatened? What if you find a situation or person annoying, but there's no real reason to attack the person or to defend yourself? Using a serene or peaceful facial expression and an open, relaxed body position will communicate to your brain that you're safe and things are going to be okay. When your brain receives this message, your anger will very likely start to diminish.

- ## Jeff's Story

When Jeff was stuck in traffic or behind a slow driver, he would yell and scream, rev the engine, make rude gestures, and try desperately to move ahead of other cars or pass the slow driver. When he decided to use opposite action in these situations, Jeff drove at or only slightly above the speed limit, relaxed his grip on the steering wheel, and wore a more relaxed facial expression. These seemingly small changes made a huge difference in how angry Jeff felt when he was inconvenienced while driving. Furthermore, Jeff found that he got home or to work just as quickly without all of the angry behavior. As a result, he gradually became less and less frustrated with the hassles of driving.

5. Do the Opposite Action Fully and Mindfully

Opposite action tends to work best when you jump into it fully with body and mind (Linehan 1993a, 2015). You need to perform the action with your full attention. For example, if you are using the skill of being compassionate, this skill will be far more effective if you bring your full attention to the activity at hand. It can be useful to keep track of how mindful you are when you try an opposite action. Pay attention to whether your mind is focused on what you are doing or if it's wandering somewhere else. Afterward, consider if you put your full effort into the opposite action. Were you giving it your full attention, or were you only doing it halfway? It's important to figure out if you tend to do an opposite action without your full attention. That way the next time you're in a similar situation, you can remind yourself to really immerse yourself in the opposite action and to be fully present. Then, see if you can tell any difference between doing the opposite action mindfully versus mindlessly. Was it more effective?

Moving Forward

In this chapter, we reviewed one of the most powerful skills for modifying anger—opposite action. As we discussed, opposite action involves five key steps: identify what emotion you are experiencing, determine if your anger is effective, describe your action urges, choose an opposite action, and do the opposite action fully and mindfully. Although this skill is more complex than some of the others we describe, it is worth the effort. It will become easier to use if you practice it regularly. Even if you began practicing all of the skills we discussed so far, you will probably slip up and act out of anger in the heat of the moment. Rest assured that this is perfectly normal. In the next chapter we discuss skills you can use when you slip up and do or say things that you later regret.

CHAPTER 11

Expressing Anger Effectively

As you may remember from chapter 4, many of the situations and experiences that bring up anger involve other people: being told no; not having your opinions, wants, or needs considered; or having someone disagree with you. Let's face it, as much as other people can be a source of support, joy, and connectedness, they can also be a source of frustration and anger. This makes a lot of sense when you consider that being prevented from reaching a goal is one of the most common cues for anger. Although many things can get in the way of reaching a goal, such as a computer malfunction, loss of electricity, or bad weather, other people are often the culprits. Other people can do things (often unintentionally) that make it harder for us to achieve our goals. All people have their own desires, goals, opinions, and struggles, so it's only natural that these will sometimes conflict with ours. When that happens and your anger is cued by another person, expressing how you feel and what you need is a good way to regulate your anger. Therefore, it's important to learn how to express anger effectively.

When it comes to expressing anger effectively, you need to consider both what you want to say and how to say it effectively. Figuring out what your anger is telling you and using that information to assert your needs is one of the best strategies for regulating anger. The trick is to do so effectively, though, so that the other person is willing to stick around and hear what you have to say. The skills in this chapter will help you accomplish these goals.

TIPS FOR EXPRESSING ANGER EFFECTIVELY

As painful as it can be to experience anger, it can be just as painful to have anger directed toward you. Most people don't enjoy being the source or object of someone else's anger, and a natural instinct is to try to avoid such situations. Therefore, it can be very difficult to express anger in such a way that other people remain open to listening to you and really hearing what you have to say. The good news is that there are several skills you can use to express anger effectively and increase the likelihood that people will listen to you.

Use Nonjudgmental Language

Nonjudgmental language can help you communicate your emotions effectively and avoid arguments, debates, and conflict. Most people get defensive or shut down if someone uses judgmental language, such as "bad," "wrong," "selfish," or "mean," to describe them or their behavior. And if this happens, they are far less open to hearing the rest of what the person has to say. Another downside of judgmental language is that it is inherently subjective and open to debate. It's difficult to argue with someone who is objectively describing the facts of what happened and how they felt, such as "When you said I was lazy, I felt hurt." It's much easier to argue with judgments and opinions, such as "You were a jerk last night." People could easily come up with counterarguments for this statement, but it's hard to argue with actual facts, such as the fact that someone said you were "lazy."

Therefore, one of the best ways to make people open to hearing what you have to say is to use the mindfulness skill of objectively labeling your experience (Linehan 1993b, 2015) to describe what angered you. Describe the situation in a neutral, matter-of-fact way, letting go of any evaluations or judgments. Stick to the facts. Focus on describing only what you observed, rather than adding in your interpretations, judgments, or opinions. For example, rather than judging the person as "rude" or "mean," objectively describe what that person said or did and how it made you feel. Sticking to the facts and avoiding judgmental language will help you communicate your anger more effectively.

As helpful as this skill can be, it's not always easy to use, especially when you're first learning it. Judgments have a way of sneaking into people's descriptions of things. As we mentioned in chapter 9, all humans use judgments. Thus, the first step in avoiding judgments is to become aware of them. One way to do this is to identify judgments in your descriptions of things. To practice this, write about a recent situation that angered you.

Write about it as you would describe it to a good friend. Next, go back through your description and circle or highlight all of the judgments and opinions you can identify. Many people find that they need to repeat this part of the exercise several times to identify all of the judgments and opinions that are present. Finally, see if you can rewrite the description in an objective way, replacing the judgments and opinions with objective descriptions of exactly what happened. You can also use exercises 9.1 and 9.2 in chapter 9 to practice this skill.

Use a Nonaggressive Tone and Demeanor

You've probably heard the old saying "You can catch more flies with honey than with vinegar." There's a lot of truth to that statement, both in terms of catching flies and expressing anger effectively. People are generally more willing to listen when you speak calmly and respectfully. If you approach someone in an aggressive manner, the natural response is to shut down, leave, or act aggressively in return. Regardless, it's unlikely that the person will be open to hearing what you have to say. If you express anger in a nonaggressive way, using a calm tone of voice and nonthreatening demeanor and body language, the person will be more likely to listen. Now, don't get us wrong. We're not saying you can't be firm or direct or express how you feel. We're not suggesting that you pretend you're happy or that you ignore your anger. We're simply suggesting that people will be more willing to listen to what you have to say if you say it without raising your voice or using aggressive gestures.

One of the barriers to using this skill is that many people don't know what they look like or how they sound when they express anger. It's difficult to know how you come across to others. For this reason, it can be helpful to practice this skill in front of a mirror or to record yourself expressing anger. Watching and listening to yourself as you express anger will give you a much better understanding of your tone of voice, posture, and demeanor and allow you to practice using nonaggressive body language and tone. You could also ask a trusted friend, loved one, or therapist to watch you practice this skill and then give you feedback on how you sound and look. The more you practice expressing anger in a calm and nonthreatening way, the more effective you'll be when you're talking to the person you're angry with.

USING YOUR ANGER TO ASSERT YOUR NEEDS

Now that we've offered some tips for expressing your anger effectively, it's time to focus on what your anger is telling you and how to use that information to assert your needs. Using anger to assert your needs is one of the best strategies for regulating this emotion. Once you use the information an emotion is providing you, the emotion is more likely to pass. What's more, using anger to tackle your problems head-on can help you get what you need. Although using your anger in this way may seem like a daunting task, there is an entire set of DBT skills devoted to helping people assert their needs while also maintaining good relationships with others (Linehan 1993b, 2015).

Figure Out What You Need

The first step in using your anger to assert your needs is to figure out exactly what those needs are (Linehan 1993b, 2015). It's hard to communicate effectively if you aren't sure what you want or what you're asking for. So spend some time figuring out what your anger is telling you and what you'd like the other person to say or do. Do you want the person to do something different in the future or to change her or his behavior in some way? Do you want the person to understand where you're coming from and apologize for some action? Do you want the person to work with you to come up with a solution to an ongoing problem? The first step is to figure out exactly what your needs are in this interaction.

Develop a Script for Expressing Your Anger and Asserting Your Needs

The next step is to develop a script for asserting your needs, or asking for what you want. Begin by explaining the situation that angered you as clearly and objectively as possible. The mindfulness skill of objectively labeling your experience (Linehan 1993b, 2015) will be incredibly helpful for this. Describing the situation objectively and refraining from using judgmental language will provide a good first impression. This is your opportunity to set the tone for the conversation.

Next, tell the person how you feel about the situation using "I feel" and "I think" statements. Because the focus of this chapter is on expressing anger effectively, it's likely that at least one of the emotions you describe will be anger related. Although you could just say, "I feel angry," keep in mind that there are all kinds of words to describe anger, including "irritation," "aggravation," "frustration," and "rage." Therefore, you want to select the word that best captures your level and type of anger. If you're experiencing mild anger, you could say "I feel frustrated" or "I feel annoyed." You may find it helpful to look back at chapter 1 to remind yourself of the different varieties of anger and their intensity.

Another thing to keep in mind when describing how you feel is that certain anger-related words are more intense than others, and it's generally easier for others to hear less intense words. Therefore, even if you're feeling incredibly angry, to the point of rage, we recommend saying "I feel angry" rather than "I feel enraged" because the listener will find the first statement easier to tolerate. This doesn't mean you can't be true to yourself or express how you feel. We just want you to consider how the words will sound to the other person and if there are other words you can use that are still accurate but easier to hear. Along the same lines, if the situation brought about softer or more vulnerable emotions in addition to anger, such as sadness, fear, or embarrassment, it can be helpful to express those too. Expressing more vulnerable emotions along with anger can help you get your point across and elicit empathy from others.

The next step is to state your needs and what you want. Make sure you are as specific as possible and state directly what you want the person to do. This is where the work you did to figure out your needs comes into play. When you're describing your needs and what you want to the other person, it's important to be as clear as possible. Don't assume that some things go without saying. Even if you think the person knows what you want or need, or if you've told the person these things in the past, it's important to spell things out clearly and directly. The more specific you can be, the more likely it is the other person will understand.

The last step in developing the script is to describe exactly how the other person will benefit from doing what you ask and giving you what you need. Not all basic assertiveness training covers this, but we believe it is incredibly important. The goal is to make it clear to the other person upfront that there are benefits to doing what you ask—that giving you what you need can be a win-win situation (or at least can help the other person in some important ways). For example, you could explain to the person that doing what you ask will make your relationship stronger or reduce conflict or make you more willing to say yes to their requests. See the *Skills Training Manual for Treating Borderline Personality Disorder* (Linehan 1993b) or the *DBT Skills Training Manual* (Linehan 2015) for more specifics on the skills in this chapter.

Plan Ahead and Practice

Once you've prepared your script, there are a couple more steps you need to take to be as prepared as possible to express your anger effectively. First, you need to think about compromises you're willing to make if the other person cannot or will not give you everything you want (Linehan 1993b, 2015). Unfortunately, no matter how skillfully you express your anger and assert your needs, the other person may not be able or willing to do what you request. Therefore, once you've figured out what you want, it's important to determine if you're willing to compromise on any of your requests. Thinking this through ahead of time is really important. It can be hard to consider all of the consequences of various options when you are in the middle of an interaction and experiencing anger. Identifying acceptable compromises ahead of time will make the process of asserting your needs go as smoothly as possible.

Second, it's important to practice your script again and again until you feel comfortable with it. Practice it as many times as you need. This is also a useful time to practice using a nonaggressive tone and demeanor. Practice your script in front of a mirror or with a close friend or loved one. Record yourself practicing the script and then listen to the recording to evaluate how your voice sounds and how the words come across. Don't forget to pay attention to your nonverbal behaviors, such as tone of voice and facial expressions, in addition to the words you are using.

Exercise 11.1   Steps for Expressing Your Anger and Asserting Your Needs Effectively

1. Figure out what you need and clarify your goals for the interaction. Ask yourself the following: *What is my anger telling me? What do I want out of this interaction? What do I want this person to do or say? What changes, if any, do I want this person to make?* Write your answers below.

    _____

    _____

    _____

    _____

    _____

2. Develop a script for expressing your anger and asserting your needs. Be sure to complete each of the following sections:

    First, explain the situation that angered you. Describe the situation as clearly and objectively as possible. Avoid judgments and opinions in your explanation.

    _____

    _____

    _____

    _____

Second, explain how you feel about the situation using "I feel" and "I think" statements. Choose the words that best describe your feelings of anger, such as "irritated," "frustrated," "aggravated," "angry," or "enraged."

_____

_____

_____

_____

_____

Third, state your needs and what you want. Be as specific as possible.

_____

_____

_____

_____

Fourth, clarify upfront how giving you what you need or want will benefit the other person.

_____

_____

_____

_____

_____

Fifth, identify compromises you are willing to make. Even if you don't end up needing to compromise, it is good to know how far you are willing to bend in order to reach an agreement.

_____

_____

_____

_____

_____

3. Practice this script until you feel comfortable with it. Try it out in front of a mirror or with a close friend or loved one. Record yourself practicing the script in order to hear what you sound like. Pay attention to nonverbal behaviors, such as tone of voice and facial expressions, in addition to the words you are using.

4. When you feel prepared, approach the other person and express your anger. Keep in mind that this skill, just like all the others in this book, gets easier with practice. It may also be helpful to pair this skill with some of the skills in chapter 8 for reducing the intensity of anger, such as slowing your breathing, lowering your body temperature, and letting go of anger-related thoughts.

Moving Forward

Expressing your anger in a healthy and effective way is one of the best ways to manage anger and keep it from intensifying. Using anger to address problems and get your needs met can put you in touch with the benefits and upsides of anger. And expressing your anger effectively can protect you from its downsides. The skills in this chapter focused on using anger to figure out and assert your needs in effective ways. Indeed, the effective expression of anger has two main parts: what you say and how you say it. Although expressing anger effectively will become easier with practice, it takes time for the skills to become second nature and easy to implement on the spot. Therefore, when you are first learning these skills, we recommend preparing in advance and planning out what you want to say and how you plan to say it.

In this book, we've taught you skills for identifying and understanding your patterns of anger, reducing the intensity of anger, controlling behavior when you're feeling angry (so you don't make things worse), managing anger-related thoughts, and expressing anger effectively. However, it's equally important to have skills for managing the aftermath of anger episodes. No matter how many skills you use or how effective they are, the aftereffects of intense anger can be just as difficult to manage as the anger itself. Skills for effectively managing the aftermath of anger episodes are described in the next and final chapter.

CHAPTER 12

Managing the Aftermath of Anger

Managing the aftermath of an anger episode is one of the most challenging and painful tasks involved in learning how to manage anger effectively. The aftereffects of anger—from the impact of this emotion on your energy levels and emotional and physical state to the consequences of things you said or did out of anger—tend to linger long after the initial emotion has passed. For these reasons it is helpful to know how to deal with the aftereffects.

MANAGING THE AFTEREFFECTS OF INTENSE EMOTIONS

Because emotions affect the entire body, experiencing a very intense emotion for a prolonged period of time can really take a toll. This is especially true for an emotion that's as energizing and activating as anger. Once the rush of adrenaline subsides and the anger passes, you'll probably feel worn-out and depleted. At times like these, one of the best things you can do for yourself is to care for your body. The good news is that there is an entire set of DBT skills designed to help you do just that.

Self-Soothing Skills

One of the best ways to care for your body is to soothe yourself physically (Linehan 1993b, 2015). Self-soothing skills can help you replenish your body's resources and return to a calmer state. The physical toll of intense anger can put you on edge and leave you vulnerable to more intense anger or other emotions. Soothing yourself physically in the wake of intense anger can reduce your risk for both. Think of it as a prevention strategy: the quicker you can recover from an episode of intense anger, the less vulnerable you'll be to intense anger in the future.

The idea behind self-soothing skills is to introduce a comforting sensation to the five senses: touch, taste, smell, sight, and sound. The best self-soothing strategies are those that activate more than one sense at a time. In chapter 7, we described focusing on the five senses as a distraction skill, not a self-soothing skill. That wasn't a mistake. Focusing on your senses can work either way. The difference is the kind of sensation you are trying to create. In the case of distraction, you want to create really intense sensations that capture your attention and take your mind off your anger. When you use your senses to soothe yourself, you want to create gentle sensations that calm you. There are many sensations that people find soothing and comforting (Linehan 1993b, 2015). Many of these were taken from our book *The Dialectical Behavior Therapy Skills Workbook for Anxiety* (Chapman, Gratz, and Tull 2011).

Touch. Introduce sensations that soothe your body and feel good against your skin. Put on soft clothing, such as a fuzzy sweater, flannel shirt, cotton sweatshirt or T-shirt, warm fleece, or silk shirt. Focus on the feeling of the fabric against your skin. Take a warm bubble bath or hot shower, or sit in a hot tub. Focus on the feeling of the water against your skin. Sit in a sauna or relax in the sun, focusing on the warmth against your skin. Get a massage, or give yourself a massage. Pet your cat or dog (or other animal), focusing on the feel of the fur against your skin. Hug a friend or loved one. Wrap yourself up in a warm, fluffy blanket and curl up on a comfortable chair or in bed. Sit in front of a fire and focus on the warmth you feel.

Taste. Eat your favorite comfort food, such as mashed potatoes, macaroni and cheese, cinnamon buns, sushi, or freshly baked bread. Sip a cup of hot cocoa or tea or some other hot drink. On a hot day, eat a popsicle or an ice cream bar. Eat dark chocolate or a piece of fresh fruit and focus on the flavors.

Smell. Burn incense or light a scented candle and focus on the scents that are released. Apply scented lotion to your skin and inhale the aroma. Go to a flower shop, botanical garden, or arboretum and breathe in the scents of the flowers. Inhale the aroma of lavender or vanilla. Go outside and breathe in fresh air. Bake cookies or fresh bread and breathe in the aroma. Smell fresh coffee beans or brew fresh coffee. Cut fresh herbs or open jars of spices and breathe in deeply. Light a fire and focus on the smell of the smoke and burning wood.

Sight. Look at pictures of loved ones or a favorite vacation spot. Look at pictures of things you find relaxing, such as a beach, a sunset, or a beautiful mountain. Go to the beach and watch the waves hit the sand. Watch a sunset. Watch clouds in the sky or leaves rustling in the breeze. Watch your pet or children play or sleep. Watch the flames of a fire or candle move and dance in the air.

Sound. Listen to relaxing music, birds singing, or children playing. Take a walk through the woods or around your neighborhood and listen to the sounds of nature. Sit outside at dusk and listen to the crickets. Go to the beach and listen to the sound of waves crashing on the shore. Light a fire and listen to the pop and crackle of the wood.

As you practice these skills, be sure to focus your attention completely on your sensations. Stay in the moment. If you find yourself getting distracted, notice that, and then turn your attention back to your senses.

Exercise 12.1   Identifying Self-Soothing Skills

For each of your senses, see if you can come up with five self-soothing skills that will work for you.

TOUCH

1. _____

2. _____

3. _____

4. _____

5. _____

TASTE

1. _____

2. _____

3. _____

4. _____

5. _____

SMELL

1. _____

2. _____

3. _____

4. _____

5. _____

SIGHT

1. _____

2. _____

3. _____

4. _____

5. _____

SOUND

1. _____

2. _____

3. _____

4. _____

5. _____

Once you've identified some self-soothing skills that may work for you, it's time to put them to the test. The next time you're on the other side of an anger episode and notice that you feel depleted or on edge, try one of these skills. Use exercise 12.2 to keep track of how well each skill you identified works for you.

Exercise 12.2   Practicing Self-Soothing After Anger Episodes

Use this worksheet to track your use of self-soothing skills and figure out which ones work best for you. First, in the column labeled "Self-Soothing Skill," write in the skills you identified in exercise 12.1. Then, the next time you're recovering from an episode of anger— right after the anger has passed—rate how tense and worn-out you feel on a scale from 0 (completely calm and full of energy) to 10 (incredibly tense, on edge, and depleted) and write this rating in the "Discomfort Before" column. Next, try one of the self-soothing skills you listed and then immediately rate your tension and energy level again; write this number in the "Discomfort After" column. Tracking your use of these skills will help you figure out which of the skills work best for you.

Self-Soothing Skill	Discomfort Before (0 to 10)	Discomfort After (0 to 10)
Touch		
1.		
2.		
3.		
4.		
5.		
Taste		
1.		
2.		
3.		
4.		
5.		

Smell		
1.		
2.		
3.		
4.		
5.		
Sight		
1.		
2.		
3.		
4.		
5.		
Sound		
1.		
2.		
3.		
4.		
5.		

MANAGING THE AFTEREFFECTS OF ANGER ACTIONS

Not only can intense anger have aftereffects on your body and energy levels; the things you do or say when you're angry can have aftereffects as well. One of the most difficult things to do as you're learning to manage your anger can be facing the consequences of your anger actions and their impact on those you care about. Even as you continue to practice the skills in this book, there will probably be times when you do or say things out of anger that you later regret. Therefore, it's important to learn skills for managing the negative consequences of harmful anger actions.

Doing something you regret is a recipe for all kinds of distressing and painful emotions, such as remorse, shame, and guilt. Two of the emotions people experience most frequently following ineffective or harmful anger actions are guilt and shame. Although people often use these words interchangeably, there are important distinctions between the two. Guilt stems from negative evaluations of our behaviors or actions. It tends to come up when people evaluate their behaviors negatively. And guilt can be a really helpful emotion. It can motivate people to not repeat certain behaviors or to repair the damage to relationships caused by their actions. Guilt about expressing anger ineffectively can motivate people to express anger differently in the future, to use skills to better manage their anger, or to apologize to the person they hurt. All of these can be helpful ways of managing the aftereffects of anger outbursts.

Shame, on the other hand, is far less helpful. Rather than stemming from negative evaluations of specific things you said or did, shame stems from negative evaluations of yourself as a whole. As a result, shame leads to self-hatred and low self-worth (which is never useful!), and it can actually get in the way of changing problematic behaviors or making amends. Think about it. If you think that you're a decent person who sometimes does things that aren't okay, you may experience guilt and may be motivated to change the behaviors you don't like. On the other hand, if you think you're a terrible person all around, it's probably hard to imagine that things could ever change. When you feel shame, it's easy to believe that it's pointless to work on changing your behavior. Because guilt and shame are such different emotions, the skills for managing them are different too.

Skills for Managing Guilt

As we mentioned above, feelings of guilt can be helpful. You can think of guilt as a signal to make amends for your behavior and repair any relationships that were hurt as a result. Therefore, some of the most helpful skills for managing guilt involve acting on the emotion directly (Linehan 1993b, 2015).

Acknowledge the negative consequences of your behaviors. It's hard to make amends without first acknowledging how your actions have negatively affected others. Therefore, doing so is the first step in managing guilt effectively. The next time you feel guilt about the ways you acted when angry, take some time to figure out the negative consequences of your actions for others. You may want to use exercise 7.2 to assist you with this.

Apologize. Once you've figured out how your actions hurt others, use that information to apologize for those actions (Linehan 1993b, 2015). Taking responsibility for your behavior, demonstrating that you are taking it seriously, expressing remorse for your actions, and saying you're sorry can go a long way in repairing any damage that was done. These actions demonstrate to others that you care about how your behaviors affected them.

Repair and strengthen the relationship. Repairing the relationships that were hurt by your actions is one of the best skills for managing guilt related to anger actions (Linehan 1993b, 2015). You can think of this skill as an extension of apologizing. Whereas apologizing helps get the relationship back to where it was before the anger actions, this skill involves working to get the relationship to a better, stronger place than where it started (Linehan 1993b, 2015). The next time you lash out at someone or act on anger in ways you regret, try to figure out what you can do to make the relationship even stronger than it was. Do something kind for that person, or go out of your way to bring that person joy or pleasure. Think about what's missing in the relationship and what would make it stronger. If you don't see the person very often, plan an outing or get-together. If you've been distracted by the stress in your life, set aside time to focus all of your attention on this person. Repairing and making the relationship stronger than it was is an excellent way to regulate guilt.

Let go of the guilt and move on. Once you've used your guilt to take responsibility for your actions, apologize, and repair the relationship, it's time to let go of the guilt and move forward (Linehan 1993b, 2015). You can think of this skill as the last step in managing guilt. As helpful as this emotion can be, it's only helpful when it motivates you to engage in positive behaviors. Once you've used your guilt in the ways detailed above, however, it has

Managing the Aftermath of Anger

served its purpose. It isn't helpful if it hangs around after you've apologized and repaired your relationships. So once you've taken these steps to manage your guilt, it's time to forgive yourself and let go of this emotion.

Skills for Managing Shame

Objectively label your experience. One way to decrease shame is to use the mindfulness skill of objectively labeling your experience (Linehan 1993b, 2015) to stick to the facts of what happened. Refrain from judging yourself or using inflammatory language such as "evil" or "horrible" to describe yourself or your behaviors; these things will only make you feel worse. Instead, describe in an objective way what you did when you were angry and what the consequences were. This skill will minimize self-judgments and the feelings of shame that go along with these judgments. Labeling your experience objectively will also allow you to focus on more productive and helpful responses, such as what you can do to repair the relationships that were damaged or skills you can use to manage your anger more effectively in the future.

Acting opposite to shame action urges. Another skill that can be helpful for managing shame is opposite action (Linehan 1993b, 2015). In chapter 10, we focused on ways you can use the skill of opposite action to regulate ineffective anger. The same principles apply here. One way to modulate emotions is to act in ways that are counter to the action urges that go along with the emotion. For shame, the action urges are to hide, avoid, shut down, and self-punish. Therefore, if you want to reduce feelings of shame, the best strategy is to approach the people who were affected by your anger and use the skills discussed earlier to make amends and repair any damage that was done. Look them in the eye. Continue to reach out to others and surround yourself with people you care about. Do your best to avoid isolating yourself from others. As difficult as it may be to resist urges to avoid other people, doing so will help you reduce feelings of shame.

Practicing Self-Compassion

People who struggle with anger often have negative judgments about anger, which can cause them to judge themselves for experiencing it. Just the experience of anger itself—even if it is managed effectively and expressed skillfully—can result in self-judgments and shame. The problem with this is that anger is a normal, unavoidable human emotion. Therefore, beating yourself up or judging yourself as "bad" or "evil" for feeling anger isn't going to stop it from occurring. In fact, doing so will only make you feel worse. And anything that makes you feel worse and increases feelings of shame is only going to make you more vulnerable to intense anger in the future. Therefore, the next time you experience anger, treat yourself with compassion and kindness. Rather than beating yourself up for having a normal human emotion, treat yourself with love and respect. There are many ways to practice self-compassion.

Do something nice for yourself. Even if you don't feel loving toward yourself in the moment, you can behave lovingly by doing something nice for yourself. Give yourself a gift, treat yourself to your favorite meal or snack, watch your favorite television show or movie, or practice one of the self-soothing skills we described above. Acting as if you love and respect yourself is one way to elicit those feelings and increase self-compassion.

Validate your anger. If you notice that you're judging yourself for feeling anger, shift your attention to the information your anger provided you. Remind yourself that all emotions—including anger—are valid and important and serve a purpose. Figure out what your anger was telling you and the purpose it served. Approach your anger as a friend or helpful guide rather than an enemy. Although it's important to be aware of the downsides of some anger urges, it's equally important to respect your anger and the benefits it can have.

Focus on your strengths and positive characteristics. Self-judgments can quickly take on a life of their own and spiral out of control. Although you may begin by judging yourself for experiencing anger, before you know it you may be judging yourself for all sorts of emotions and behaviors. Focusing on your positive behaviors and the things you like about yourself can counteract this spiral. For example, focus on all of the things you do that result in positive consequences for others. Think about steps you've been taking to improve your life and gain more skills. Recognize your accomplishments. Focus on the parts of yourself that you appreciate. Focusing on your positive characteristics and strengths can be very encouraging and can motivate you to make important changes. In contrast, beating yourself up for feeling anger or expressing it ineffectively can be demoralizing, making it less likely that you'll take steps to change.

Moving Forward

In this chapter, we focused on skills you can use to manage the aftermath of anger. No matter how many skills you use or how effectively you use them, the aftereffects of intense anger tend to linger long after the emotion passes. From the toll that any intense emotion takes on the body to the guilt and shame people feel when they lash out at others or act on anger in ways they regret, the aftereffects of anger can be just as difficult to manage as the anger itself. That's why it's so important to know how to take care of yourself and your relationships in the aftermath of an anger episode.

Think of the skills in this chapter as a road map to treating yourself and others with kindness and respect. No matter what you do when you're angry or how guilty you feel, beating yourself up is only going to make things worse. So have compassion for yourself. Recognize the effort you're putting into learning how to manage your anger more effectively and the time and energy it takes. Give yourself credit for reading this book, learning about your anger, and practicing the skills we've discussed. Focus on the progress you've made, and the ways your life will improve if you continue to work on your anger. And, when you do act out of anger in hurtful or ineffective ways, take responsibility for your actions, apologize for your behavior, and focus on improving your relationships and making them stronger.

References

American Psychiatric Association. 2013. *Diagnostic and Statistical Manual of Mental Disorders: DSM-5.* 5th ed. Washington, DC: American Psychiatric Association.

Bourne, E. J. 1995. *The Anxiety and Phobia Workbook.* 2nd ed. Oakland, CA: New Harbinger Publications.

Brach, T. 2003. *Radical Acceptance.* New York, NY: Bantam Books.

Bushman, B. J. 2002. "Does Venting Anger Feed or Extinguish the Flame? Catharsis, Rumination, Distraction, Anger, and Aggressive Responding." *Personality and Social Psychology Bulletin* 28 (6): 724–31.

Chapman, A. L., K. L. Gratz, and M. T. Tull. 2011. *The Dialectical Behavior Therapy Skills Workbook for Anxiety: Breaking Free from Worry, Panic, PTSD, and Other Anxiety Symptoms.* Oakland, CA: New Harbinger Publications.

Cuijpers, P., A. Van Straten, and L. Warmerdam. 2007. "Behavioral Activation Treatments of Depression: A Meta-Analysis." *Clinical Psychology Review* 27 (3): 318–26.

Deffenbacher, J. L. 1999. "Cognitive-Behavioral Conceptualization and Treatment of Anger." *Journal of Clinical Psychology* 55 (3): 295–309.

Epstein, L. J., D. Kristo, P. J. Strollo Jr., N. Friedman, A. Malhotra, S. P. Patil et al. 2009. "Clinical Guidelines for the Evaluation, Management, and Long-Term Care of Obstructive Sleep Apnea in Adults." *Journal of Clinical Sleep Medicine* 5 (3): 263–76.

Gratz, K. L., and A. L. Chapman. 2009. *Freedom from Self-Harm: Overcoming Self-Injury with Skills from DBT and Other Treatments.* Oakland, CA: New Harbinger Publications.

Gross, J. J. 1998. "The Emerging Field of Emotion Regulation: An Integrative Review." *Review of General Psychology* 2 (3): 271–99.

Gross, J. J. 2014. *Handbook of Emotion Regulation.* 2nd ed. New York, NY: Guilford Press.

Hofmann, S.G., A. Asnaani, I. J. J. Vonk, A. T. Sawyer, and A. Fang. 2012. "The Efficacy of Cognitive Behavioral Therapy: A Review of Meta-Analyses." *Cognitive Therapy and Research* 36(5): 427–440.

Kabat-Zinn, J. 1990. *Full Catastrophe Living: Using the Wisdom of Your Body and Mind to Face Stress, Pain, and Illness.* New York, NY: Delacorte Press.

Kassinove, H. 1995. *Anger Disorders: Definition, Diagnosis, and Treatment.* Washington, DC: Taylor & Francis.

Lazarus, R. S. 1991. *Emotion and Adaptation.* New York, NY: Oxford University Press.

Lieb, K., M. C. Zanarini, C. Schmahl, M. M. Linehan, and M. Bohus. 2004. "Seminar Section: Borderline Personality Disorder." *Lancet* 364: 453–461.

Linehan, M. M. 1993a. *Cognitive-Behavioral Treatment of Borderline Personality Disorder.* New York, NY: Guilford Press.

Linehan, M. M. 1993b. *Skills Training Manual for Treating Borderline Personality Disorder.* 1st ed. New York, NY: Guilford Press.

Linehan, M. M. 2007. *Opposite Action: Changing Emotions You Want to Change.* Behavioral Tech, LLC, instructional video.

Linehan, M. M. 2015. *DBT Skills Training Manual.* 2nd ed. New York, NY: Guilford Press.

Lokhorst, A. M., C. Werner, H. Staats, E. van Dijk, and J. L. Gale. 2013. "Commitment and Behavior Change: A Meta-Analysis and Critical Review of Commitment-Making Strategies in Environmental Research." *Environment and Behavior* 45(1): 3–34.

Marlatt, G. A., and J. R. Gordon. 1985. *Relapse Prevention: Maintenance Strategies in the Treatment of Addictive Behaviors.* New York, NY: Guilford Press.

Mauss, I. B., R. W. Levenson, L. McCarter, F. H. Wilhelm, and J. J. Gross. 2005. "The Tie That Binds? Coherence Among Emotion Experience, Behavior, and Physiology." *Emotion* 5 (2): 175–90.

Mazzucchelli, T., R. Kane, and C. Rees. 2009. "Behavioral Activation Treatments for Depression in Adults: A Meta-Analysis and Review." *Clinical Psychology: Science and Practice* 16 (4): 383–411.

Miller, W. R., and S. Rollnick. 2012. *Motivational Interviewing: Helping People Change.* 3rd ed. New York, NY: Guilford Press.

Muraven, M., and R. F. Baumeister. 2000. "Self-Regulation and Depletion of Limited Resources: Does Self-Control Resemble a Muscle?" *Psychological Bulletin* 126 (2): 247–59.

Nhat Hanh, T. 1991. *Peace Is Every Step: The Path of Mindfulness in Everyday Life.* New York, NY: Bantam Books.

Nolen-Hoeksema, S. 1991. "Responses to Depression and Their Effects on the Duration of Depressive Episodes." *Journal of Abnormal Psychology* 100 (4): 569–82.

Ochsner, K. N., and J. J. Gross. 2014. "The Neural Bases of Emotion and Emotion Regulation: A Valuation Perspective." In *Handbook of Emotion Regulation,* 2nd ed., edited by J. J. Gross. New York, NY: Guilford Press.

Peled, M., and M. M. Moretti. 2007. "Rumination on Anger and Sadness in Adolescence: Fueling of Fury and Deepening of Despair." *Journal of Clinical Child and Adolescent Psychology* 36 (1): 66–75.

Prochaska, J. O., and C. C. DiClemente. 1984. *The Transtheoretical Approach: Crossing Traditional Boundaries of Therapy.* Malabar, FL: Krieger Publishing Company.

Romanov, K., M. Hatakka, E. Keskinen, H. Laaksonen, J. Kaprio, R. J. Rose, and M. Koskenvuo. 1994. "Self-Reported Hostility and Suicidal Acts, Accidents, and Accidental Deaths: A Prospective Study of 21,443 Adults Aged 25 to 59." *Psychosomatic Medicine* 56 (4): 328–36.

Robins, C. J., and A. L. Chapman 2004. "Dialectical Behavior Therapy: Current Status, Recent Developments, and Future Directions." *Journal of Personality Disorders* 18 (1): 73–89.

Smart, R. G., R. E. Mann, and G. Stoduto. 2003. "The Prevalence of Road Rage: Estimates from Ontario." *Canadian Journal of Public Health* 94 (4): 247–50.

Stoffers, J. M., B. A. Völlm, G. Rücker, A. Timmer, N. Huband, and K. Lieb. 2012. "Psychological Therapies for People with Borderline Personality Disorder." *Cochrane Database of Systematic Reviews* 8: CD005652.

Suls, J., and J. Bunde. 2005. "Anger, Anxiety, and Depression as Risk Factors for Cardiovascular Disease: The Problems and Implications of Overlapping Affective Dispositions." *Psychological Bulletin* 131 (2): 260–300.

Alexander L. Chapman, PhD, RPsych, is a psychologist and professor in the department of psychology at Simon Fraser University (SFU), as well as president of the DBT Centre of Vancouver. Chapman directs the Personality and Emotion Research Lab where he studies the role of emotion regulation in borderline personality disorder (BPD), self-harm, impulsivity, and other behavioral problems. His research is funded by the Canadian Institutes of Health Research. Chapman received the Young Investigator's Award of the National Education Alliance for Borderline Personality Disorder in 2007, the Canadian Psychological Association's (CPA) Scientist Practitioner Early Career Award, and a Career Investigator Award from the Michael Smith Foundation for Health Research. He has coauthored eight books—three of which received the 2012 Association for Behavioral and Cognitive Therapies (ABCT) Self-Help Book Seal of Merit Award. Chapman is committed to bringing knowledge and skills from psychological science to people who need help managing their emotions. He has been practicing mindfulness for over fifteen years, practices martial arts, and enjoys hiking, skiing, reading, and spending time with his wonderful wife and two sons.

Kim L. Gratz, PhD, is professor of psychiatry and human behavior at the University of Mississippi Medical Center where she serves as director of the division of gender, sexuality, and health, as well as director of both personality disorders research and the Dialectical Behavior Therapy (DBT) Clinic. Gratz received the Young Investigator's Award of the National Education Alliance for Borderline Personality Disorder in 2005, and the Mid-Career Investigator Award of the North American Society for the Study of Personality Disorders in 2015. She has written numerous journal articles and book chapters on borderline personality disorder (BPD), deliberate self-harm, and emotion regulation (among other topics), and is coauthor of four books on BPD, self-harm, and DBT, including *The Borderline Personality Disorder Survival Guide, Borderline Personality Disorder, Freedom from Self-Harm,* and *The Dialectical Behavior Therapy Skills Workbook for Anxiety*. Three of these books have received the Association for Behavioral and Cognitive Therapies (ABCT) Self-Help Book Seal of Merit Award. Gratz currently serves as principal investigator or coinvestigator on several large federal grants, including multiple grants from the National Institutes of Health.

Foreword writer **Marsha M. Linehan, PhD, ABPP**, is professor of psychology and director of the Behavioral Research and Therapy Clinics (BRTC) at the University of Washington in Seattle, WA. She is author of *Cognitive-Behavioral Treatment of Borderline Personality Disorder* and *Skills Training Manual for Treating Borderline Personality Disorder*.

FROM OUR PUBLISHER—

As the publisher at New Harbinger and a clinical psychologist since 1978, I know that emotional problems are best helped with evidence-based therapies. These are the treatments derived from scientific research (randomized controlled trials) that show what works. Whether these treatments are delivered by trained clinicians or found in a self-help book, they are designed to provide you with proven strategies to overcome your problem.

Therapies that aren't evidence-based—whether offered by clinicians or in books—are much less likely to help. In fact, therapies that aren't guided by science may not help you at all. That's why this New Harbinger book is based on scientific evidence that the treatment can relieve emotional pain.

This is important: if this book isn't enough, and you need the help of a skilled therapist, use the following resource to find a clinician trained in the evidence-based protocols appropriate for your problem.

Real help is available for the problems you have been struggling with. The skills you can learn from evidence-based therapies will change your life.

Matthew McKay, PhD
Publisher, New Harbinger Publications

If you need a therapist, the following organization can help you
find a therapist trained in dialectical behavior therapy (DBT).

Behavioral Tech, LLC
please visit www.behavioraltech.org and click on *Find a DBT Therapist.*

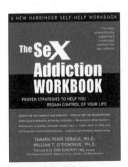

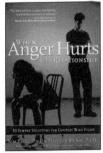

Register your **new harbinger** titles for additional benefits!

When you register your **new harbinger** title—purchased in any format, from any source—you get access to benefits like the following:

- Downloadable accessories like printable worksheets and extra content

- Instructional videos and audio files

- Information about updates, corrections, and new editions

Not every title has accessories, but we're adding new material all the time.

Access free accessories in 3 easy steps:

1. Sign in at NewHarbinger.com (or **register** to create an account).

2. Click on **register a book**. Search for your title and click the **register** button when it appears.

3. Click on the **book cover or title** to go to its details page. Click on **accessories** to view and access files.

That's all there is to it!

If you need help, visit:

NewHarbinger.com/accessories

new harbinger
CELEBRATING
40 YEARS